- INSTALL ELECTRICAL BREAKERS FOR ENTIRE SHOP WITHIN EASY REACH, CIRCUIT-RATED FOR SUFFICIENT AMPERAGE

- STOCK FIRST AID KIT WITH MATERIALS TO TREAT CUTS, GASHES, SPLINTERS, FOREIGN OBJECTS AND CHEMICALS IN EYES, AND BURNS

- HAVE TELEPHONE IN SHOP TO CALL FOR HELP

- INSTALL FIRE EXTINGUISHER RATED FOR A-, B-, AND C-CLASS FIRES

- WEAR EYE PROTECTION AT ALL TIMES

- LOCK CABINETS AND POWER TOOLS TO PROTECT CHILDREN AND INEXPERIENCED VISITORS

- USE DUST COLLECTOR TO KEEP SHOP DUST AT A MINIMUM

- WEAR SHIRT SLEEVES ABOVE ELBOWS

- WEAR CLOSE-FITTING CLOTHES

- WEAR LONG PANTS

- REMOVE WATCHES, RINGS, OR JEWELRY

- KEEP TABLE AND FENCE SURFACES WAXED AND RUST-FREE

- WEAR THICK-SOLED SHOES, PREFERABLY WITH STEEL TOES

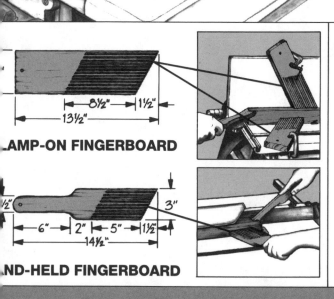

CLAMP-ON FINGERBOARD

8½" 1½"
13½"

½"
6" 2" 5" 1½"
3"
14½"

HAND-HELD FINGERBOARD

PROTECTION

WEAR FULL FACE SHIELD DURING LATHE TURNING, ROUTING, AND OTHER OPERATIONS THAT MAY THROW CHIPS

WEAR DUST MASK DURING SANDING AND SAWING

WEAR VAPOR MASK DURING FINISHING

WEAR EAR PROTECTORS DURING ROUTING, PLANING, AND LONG, CONTINUOUS POWER TOOL OPERATION

WEAR RUBBER GLOVES FOR HANDLING DANGEROUS CHEMICALS

WEAR SAFETY GLASSES OR GOGGLES AT ALL TIMES

THE WORKSHOP COMPANION™

MAKING DESKS AND BOOKCASES

TECHNIQUES FOR BETTER WOODWORKING

by Nick Engler

Rodale Press
Emmaus, Pennsylvania

If you have any questions or comments concerning this book, please write:
  Rodale Press
  Book Readers' Service
  33 East Minor Street
  Emmaus, PA 18098

About the Author: Nick Engler is an experienced wood-worker, writer, and teacher. He worked as a luthier for many years, making traditional American musical instruments before he founded *Hands On!* magazine. Today, he contributes to several woodworking magazines and teaches woodworking at the University of Cincinnati. He has written more than 30 books.

Series Editor: Jeff Day
Editors: Bob Moran
         Roger Yepsen
Copy Editors: Barbara Webb
              Carolyn Mandarano
Graphic Designer: Linda Watts
Illustrators: Mary Jane Favorite
              David Van Etten
Master Craftsman: Jim McCann
Photographer: Karen Callahan
Cover Photographer: Mitch Mandel
Proofreader: Hue Park
Indexer: Beverly Bremer
Typesetting by Computer Typography, Huber Heights, Ohio
Interior and endpaper illustrations by Mary Jane Favorite
Produced by Bookworks, Inc., West Milton, Ohio

Library of Congress Cataloging-in-Publication Data

Engler, Nick.
    Making desks and bookcases/by Nick Engler.
        p.   cm. — (The workshop companion)
    Includes index.
    ISBN 0–87596–581–4   hardcover
    1. Bookcases. 2. Desks. 3. Furniture making. I. Title
    II. Series:
    Engler, Nick.   Workshop companion.
    TT197.5.86E54   1993
    684.1'4—dc20   93–2198
                                           CIP

    4 6 8 10 9 7 5 3   hardcover

Special Thanks to:

Bounty Books
New York, New York

Larry Callahan
West Milton, Ohio

Stacy Christopher
Troy, Ohio

Colonial Williamsburg Foundation
Williamsburg, Virginia

W. R. Goehring
Gambier, Ohio

Israel Sack, Inc.
New York, New York

Smithsonian Institution
Washington, D.C.

Wertz Hardware
West Milton, Ohio

The Workshops of David T. Smith
Morrow, Ohio

CONTENTS

TECHNIQUES

PROJECTS

TECHNIQUES

1

DESK AND BOOKCASE DESIGN

Desks and bookcases are highly personal spaces. We use bookcases to hold the things that give our lives meaning — favorite books, music, and videos; treasures from past trips or events; awards and trophies; collections and artwork; photos of cherished people and places; and other reminders of who we are. And at our desks, we read (or write) the books, plan the trips, earn the awards, delight in the collections, paste the photos in scrapbooks — and pay the bills for all of them.

Because these pieces are so intimately connected with the best parts of our lives, no other woodworking projects are so thoroughly individualized. When designing a desk or bookcase, you may collect ideas from other craftsmen, but the project will reflect your own needs. It will be at least a little different than any other piece of furniture on the planet.

To give you a start, I've tried to assemble as many types, styles, and components of desks and bookcases that can be fit into one book. No doubt, you won't build any of these pieces exactly as they are shown. But you can consider the possibilities, then combine the ones that appeal to you.

TYPES OF DESKS AND BOOKCASES

When designing a desk or bookcase to suit your needs and tastes, survey the different types before picking an overall design. There are dozens, probably hundreds of types to choose from. Perhaps the best way to put these in some order is to make a *historical* survey.

A COMMON ANCESTOR

The history of desks and bookcases is, in many ways, the history of reading and writing. For thousands of years, most people couldn't read or write; consequently, they had little need for desks or bookcases. The rich and the learned had a few — as early as the seventh century, Byzantine scribes worked at slanted tables and kept their books in large standing cupboards. But it wasn't until the beginning of the Renaissance and the accompanying rise in literacy that our European ancestors began to build desks and bookcases in large numbers.

Desks and bookcases had a common forebear, the medieval *desk box,* or *lap desk. (SEE FIGURE 1-1.)* This was a portable box, designed to be set on a table or balanced on the user's lap. The slanted box lid served as both a writing surface and a reading lectern, holding papers or a book at a comfortable angle. When not in use, the book or writing materials could be stored inside the box. There was no need for a larger bookcase — books were so expensive that few people owned more than one.

That single book was most often the Bible, and in eighteenth-century America, these small bookcases became known as *Bible boxes. (SEE FIGURE 1-2.)* However, the invention of movable type in the fifteenth century and the advent of the first publishing companies in the sixteenth made books more plentiful. Personal libraries grew and so did bookcases.

1-2 Wooden boxes also served as the first bookcases. This early American *Bible box* once protected a family Bible. *Courtesy of Israel Sack, Inc., New York, New York.*

1-1 Simple desk boxes, such as this reproduction of a Shaker *lap desk,* have been used since medieval times. The slanted lid provides a comfortable writing surface, while the writing materials can be stored inside. *From The Workshops of David T. Smith, Morrow, Ohio.*

EARLY SHELVING SYSTEMS

Two pieces of medieval furniture influenced the evolution of the bookcase. The first was the *buffet* (also called a *dressoir*), a set of open standing shelves. (*SEE FIGURE 1-3.*) The buffet was used by the ruling class to display the family dishes, and the number of tiers denoted the rank of the owner. A lowly baron was allowed just two tiers, while King Henry VIII had a French-made buffet with twelve. As the medieval ages gave way to the Renaissance, buffets became more sophisticated.

Craftsmen enclosed the tiers and decorated them with carvings, moldings, and exotic veneers. These fully enclosed storage units were called *cabinets* (after the French *cabine hut,* meaning a little house or cabin), and the craftsmen who made them became known as cabinetmakers. (*SEE FIGURE 1-4.*)

1-3 Open shelves, such as this country-style *display stand,* have been used for over a thousand years. Although commonplace today, they were once status symbols for the nobility of medieval Europe, who called them *buffets* and *dressoirs.* The nobles covered the shelves with rich carpets, then displayed their fine plates on them. *From The Workshops of David T. Smith, Morrow, Ohio.*

1-4 As furniture forms evolved in Europe and America, craftsmen began to enclose open shelving units to make *cabinets* — storage space enclosed by glazed doors. This country piece was known as a *step-back cabinet,* so called because the top portion of the cabinet was not as deep as the bottom. *From The Workshops of David T. Smith, Morrow, Ohio.*

Another medieval piece that influenced the bookcase was the *cup-board*, a fixture common in every cottage of the period, no matter what the rank of its owner. This was just a board or two built into the wall to hold cups, plates, and other utensils. Eventually, craftsmen attached them to vertical supports, making *shelves*. These shelves were either hung or left freestanding. (*See Figure 1-5.*) Like the buffet, the shelves were eventually enclosed to make a storage unit for dishes, foodstuffs, and other items. This piece continues to be called by its medieval name, the *cupboard*. (*See Figure 1-6.*)

For Your Information

The old English word *scylfe* (from which *shelf* is derived) once denoted a *bench*, and the two words may have been used interchangeably. Perhaps this is because the construction of a medieval shelving unit was almost the same as a bench — there were just a few more horizontal members.

1-5 *Hanging shelves* are descended from medieval *cup-boards* — boards built into the walls of cottages and used to store cups, dishes, and other utensils. This traditional country design was known as a *whale shelf*, owing to the distinctive shape of the vertical supports. *From The Workshops of David T. Smith, Morrow, Ohio.*

1-6 While the well-to-do enclosed shelves with expensive glazed doors to make handsome cabinets, common folk surrounded them with ordinary wooden panels and retained the old name — cupboard. However, that doesn't necessarily mean that some of these pieces weren't highly crafted. This Southwest-style *hanging cupboard* is decorated with elaborate fretwork and chip carving. *Designed by Mary Jane Favorite, West Milton, Ohio.*

All of these new furniture forms — shelves, cup-boards, and cabinets — were used to hold the expand-ing libraries of Europe and its American colonies. By the seventeenth century, French cabinetmakers had begun to make the first *standing bookcases* — cabinets with glazed doors specially designed to hold books. (*SEE FIGURE 1-7.*)

1-7 After the invention of printing, books became more afford-able. Literate men and women began to collect them, and by the seven-teenth century, craftsmen were build-ing true *bookcases* — cupboards and cabinets especially designed to hold expanding libraries. This reproduc-tion of a Federal-style *standing bookcase* and contemporary *hanging bookcase* are two twentieth-century examples of the form. *Standing book-case built circa 1905, craftsman un-known. Hanging bookcase designed by the author.*

AN EXPLOSION OF PAPERWORK

As folks became more literate, they were engulfed in paperwork — correspondence, contracts, and business records. About the same time the first cabinets appeared, the small lap desk grew to become a *writing box* or *scriptor,* a chest filled with small drawers, pigeonholes, and other compartments for writing materials and records. (*See Figure 1-8.*) These writing boxes often had handles on the sides so they could be moved from location to location. Once placed on a table or stand, the front folded down to make a writing surface. An angled front, reminiscent of the slanted lids of the old lap desks, became known as a *slant front,* while a vertical front was a *fall front.*

As the burden of paperwork grew, folks could justify larger and more-permanent desks. In the seventeenth and eighteenth centuries, craftsmen married the writing box to different pieces of furniture to create several new types of *standing* desks (desks that stood on the floor). A writing box permanently attached to a stand became a *desk-on-frame.* (*See Figure 1-9.*) When mounted to a table, it was a *table desk.* (*See Figure 1-10.*) And when attached to a chest of drawers, it was called a *slant-front* or *fall-front desk* (depending on whether the front was angled or vertical). (*See Figure 1-11.*)

Craftsmen also created several new desk designs. They began to build small *writing tables* especially for correspondence and record keeping. (*See Figure 1-12.*) These usually had a single drawer beneath the work surface to hold writing materials. For clients who needed more storage space, craftsmen stretched a writing surface across two small chests of drawers to make a *kneehole desk.* (*See Figure 1-13.*) This form later evolved into the *pedestal desk,* perhaps the most useful and adaptable type of desk ever. (*See Figure 1-14.*) Soon after their introduction, pedestal desks became standard office equipment for most businesses, and they remain so today.

There were also a few new twists in bookcase design. Like the old writing boxes, they were married to various pieces of furniture to create new forms.

1-8   This fall-front country *writing box* was built to be portable. The owners of pieces like these could pack up their paperwork in the box and take it with them on their travels. When at home, the writing box usually rested on a table or stand. *Built circa 1840, craftsman unknown.*

1-9 As their clients began to request larger and more-permanent desks, craftsmen combined writing boxes with other pieces of furniture to make standing desks. Perhaps the first such desk was a writing box on a simple stand, such as this Early American slant-top *desk-on-frame*. *Courtesy of Israel Sack, Inc., New York, New York.*

1-10 When the writing box was attached to a table, it became a *table desk.* If the table was large enough to provide a comfortable work surface in front of the writing box, as is the case with this reproduction of a country table desk, the craftsman usually eliminated the fold-down front and substituted ordinary cabinet doors. *From The Workshops of David T. Smith, Morrow, Ohio.*

1-11 This Queen Anne *slant-top* desk was made by incorporating a writing box in a chest of drawers. It was a design that became extremely popular in the eighteenth and early nineteenth centuries, possibly because it offered so much storage. *Courtesy of Israel Sack, Inc., New York, New York.*

1-12 Not all standing desks offer massive amounts of storage. This delicate contemporary *writing table* provides a comfortable work surface and a single shallow drawer in which to store writing materials. *Designed by W. R. Goehring, Gambier, Ohio.*

1-13 Like a writing table, a *kneehole desk* has a broad, open work surface. However, it provides a great deal more storage. The work surface is supported by two chests of drawers, and the chests are joined at the back by a cabinet. *Courtesy of Israel Sack, Inc., New York, New York.*

1-14 The kneehole desk evolved to the *pedestal desk* when craftsmen eliminated the hard-to-reach cabinet between the two supporting chests of drawers. This proved to be one of the most popular desk types ever. The design shown was sold by Sears, Roebuck and Company around the turn of the century. *From the* 1902 Sears, Roebuck & Co. Catalogue, *courtesy of Bounty Books, New York, New York.*

One of the most popular combinations was a bookcase on top of a slant-front or fall-front desk. This became known as a *secretary*. (SEE FIGURE 1-15.) A

bookcase on legs or attached to a stand was a *cabinet-on-frame*. (SEE FIGURE 1-16.) When three or more bookcases were built side by side, with the middle cases deeper than those on the ends, the arrangement was called a *breakfront*. (SEE FIGURE 1-17.)

1-16   Bookcases were often set on stands or legs to put the books out of the reach of mice and other critters that ate them and to make them easier to reach by the critters that read them. The legs on this Victorian *cabinet-on-frame* hold the bottom shelf about 8 inches off the floor. *Built circa 1880, craftsman unknown.*

1-15   To save space, bookcases were often combined with desks in a single piece of furniture, called a *secretary*. This Chippendale secretary married a cupboard to the top of a slant-front desk. *Courtesy of Israel Sack, Inc., New York, New York.*

1-17 When making a large bookcase, craftsmen often divided it into smaller units to make it easier to build. Then, to provide visual interest, they made the middle units deeper than those on the ends. This form was known as a *breakfront*. *Courtesy of Israel Sack, Inc., New York, New York, and the Colonial Williamsburg Foundation, Williamsburg, Virginia.*

THE INDUSTRIAL AND ELECTRONIC REVOLUTIONS

Cabinetmaking became mechanized in the nineteenth century, and individual craftsmen were replaced by furniture factories. You might expect that this would have caused desk and bookcase designs to become less creative and more standardized, but the opposite happened. As furniture makers competed with each other, they introduced innovative designs. The people of this era were fascinated with mechanical marvels, and the desks and bookcases often incorporated clever devices. Perhaps the epitome of this trend was the *Wooton desk,* a patented cabinet with doors that opened to reveal a pull-out writing surface and dozens of pigeonholes, shelves, and drawers. *(SEE FIGURE 1-18.)* Wooton desks were immensely popular during the last half of the nineteenth century, but the public gradually lost interest, as they did with many other contraptions. Only a few mechanical desks and book-cases from this era are still built today. The *rolltop*

desk, a pedestal desk with dozens of pigeonholes and a tambour cover, has remained popular owing to its practicality. *(SEE FIGURE 1-19.)* The *stacking bookcase,* a set of stacking boxes with fold-up fronts, is still in demand for the same reason. *(SEE FIGURE 1-20.)*

Just as the people of the nineteenth century were fascinated with mechanical contrivances, folks in this century are captivated by electronics. Contemporary bookcases (which are now commonly referred to as *wall units,* since they often hold so much more than books) now have lighted interiors. *(SEE FIGURE 1-21.)* In many homes, the bookcase shares space with the *entertainment center,* a shelving unit designed to hold audio and video modules. *(SEE FIGURE 1-22.)* And the *computer workstation,* a special desk to hold computer components, has become commonplace in the den and office. *(SEE FIGURE 1-23.)*

1-18 The nineteenth century saw
the development of the *Wooton Desk,*
the invention of William S. Wooton
of Indianapolis, Indiana. The desk
was encased in a cabinet, which
opened to reveal a compact office
complete with filing compartments.
Wooton manufactured his desk until
the 1890s, when the invention of the
filing cabinet made it obsolete. *Cour-*
tesy of the Smithsonian Institution,
Washington, D.C., Photo No. 16594-A.

1-19 Craftsmen began to use
tambour shutters to enclose the writing boxes on the tops of standing desks in the early eighteenth century, and the first *rolltop desks* were made in France in the 1760s. But it wasn't until after the Civil War, when furniture manufacturers combined a rolltop with a pedestal desk, that the form became popular. There are two distinct types of rolltops — the *quarter-round rolltop* (shown in the photo) and the *waterfall rolltop* (shown in the drawing). *Quarter-round rolltop built circa 1930 by Imperial Desks of Evansville, Indiana. Waterfall rolltop from the 1902 Sears, Roebuck & Co. Catalogue, courtesy of Bounty Books, New York, New York.*

1-20 In the late nineteenth century, some furniture manufacturer got the bright idea that, instead of selling different sizes of bookcases, he would sell just one boxlike bookcase *module,* then let the customer buy as many modules as needed and stack them up. The result was this Victorian *stacking bookcase.* Each module had a glass door that folded up into the box. *Built circa 1880, manufacturer unknown.*

1-21 One of the most practical shelving systems to appear in recent years is the *wall unit.* The simple cabinets, usually 24 to 36 inches wide, are designed to be set next to one another. By lining up wall units, you can create as much storage as you need. Many commercial designs also have matching corner cabinets and special units to hold audio and video equipment. These contemporary units have top lighting to illuminate the open shelves. *Designed by the author.*

1-22 As electronics become more and more a part of home life, craftsmen and furniture manufacturers are making special shelving systems designed to hold televisions, radios, and other audio and video components. This contemporary *entertainment center* was built especially for audio equipment. *Designed by Larry Callahan, West Milton, Ohio.*

1-23 Just as the act of writing led to a special type of furniture called a *desk,* using a computer has given rise to a special type of desk called a *workstation.* This contemporary computer workstation holds the computer components — central processing unit, monitor, keyboard, and printer — where they can be easily seen and reached. It also provides a comfortable work surface just in case you want to do some old-fashioned writing. *Designed by Jim McCann, Phillipsburg, Ohio.*

DESK AND BOOKCASE STYLES

In addition to choosing the type of desk or bookcase you want to build, you must also decide on a *style*. Each type can be built in several different styles, which not only determine the look of a piece, but often dictate its construction. For example, when you build a bookcase in the classic Queen Anne or Federal styles, you must build wood frame doors that hold multiple small panes of glass. If you build it in a Victorian style, you can make wood frame doors with a single large pane of glass. And if you build it in the contemporary style, you can dispense with the wood frame altogether and simply hang large panes of tempered glass on special hinges.

Here are designs for a drop-front desk and a standing bookcase in nine styles that have enduring or current appeal. You can find other examples and other styles by paging through home decorating magazines and furniture design books.

1 The *Queen Anne* style first appeared in the early eighteenth century when European cabinetmakers, enamored of imported Oriental pieces, began to incorporate Japanese and Chinese design elements into their own projects. Americans followed suit a few years later. These elements included the cabriole leg, ball-and-claw foot, and shell carvings. The cyma curve, or *ogee,* was used everywhere — moldings, aprons, even the S shape of the cabriole legs. Mahogany was the preferred wood for the Queen Anne style, but craftsmen also used walnut, cherry, and figured maple.

QUEEN ANNE

2 **Immediately after the** American Revolution, there was a brief backlash against all things English — including furniture styles. American craftsmen looked to France for inspiration and adopted their neoclassic *Directoire* designs, which we now call the *Federal* style. These were functional designs based on ancient Greek and Roman forms. Americans were also influenced by two French-inspired English designers, George Hepplewhite and Thomas Sheraton. Both men published designs for light, graceful furniture. They used many straight lines — tapered legs were their hallmark.

The flat surfaces were often veneered with exotic woods and decorated with intricate inlay. Mahogany remained the favorite wood, but many Federal pieces were built from walnut, cherry, and maple.

FEDERAL

(continued) ▷

DESK AND BOOKCASE STYLES — CONTINUED

3 ***Country* cabinetmakers** worked in the towns and villages of rural America during the eighteenth and early nineteenth centuries, and their work often included elements of Queen Anne and Federal designs. The craftsmen were usually skilled — many were trained in big-city cabinet shops — but their clientele had provincial tastes and could not afford intricately worked furniture. Consequently, country furniture was much simpler than classic Queen Anne and Federal pieces, although it followed the same general lines.

Because imported mahogany was so expensive, country furniture was made from less-costly native woods such as walnut, cherry, maple, poplar, and white pine. Instead of being covered with exotic veneers, country furniture was sometimes grain-painted to look as if it had been veneered.

COUNTRY

4 **Shaker furniture developed** in the early nineteenth century out of the beliefs of a strict religious sect, the United Society of Believers in Christ's Second Appearing, also called the *Shakers*. At their height in 1850, the Shakers had 6,000 members in 19 communities across the Midwest and eastern United States. These communities made their own furniture, and because they believed "beauty rests on utility," they stripped these pieces of almost all ornament.

In doing so, they created an austere style, the forms of which depended solely on function. Shaker craftsmen worked almost all native American woods, but preferred maple, pine, and poplar.

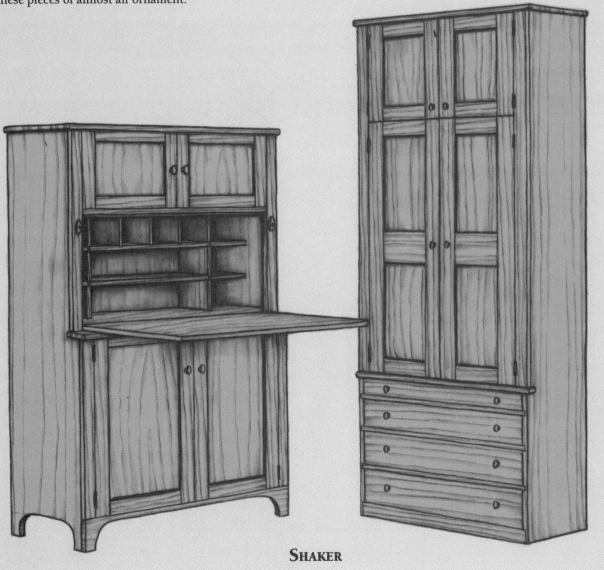

SHAKER

(continued) ▷

DESK AND BOOKCASE STYLES — CONTINUED

5 **Many people think of** Victorian furniture as the antithesis of Shaker because of its excessive ornament. Indeed, the early Victorian Revival styles — Gothic, Renaissance, and Rococo — were highly decorative. But the Victorian era was also the stage for the Industrial Revolution, and as furniture factories replaced individual cabinetmakers, furniture design and construction was simplified so it could be mass-produced. Much Victorian furniture was built in the *Grand Rapids* style, so called because many of the factories were located near Grand Rapids, Michigan. This was characterized by frame-and-panel construction, straight or lightly curved legs, band sawed pediments and aprons, applied carvings, and ornate hardware. Most Grand Rapids furniture was made from oak because it was abundant, inexpensive, and relatively stable. In fact, oak was used so extensively that some design books refer to this as *Victorian Oak, Turn-of-the-Century Oak,* or simply *Oak* furniture.

VICTORIAN OAK

6 **Arts and Crafts, or Mission,** furniture was a reaction to the industrialization of the furniture trade that began just before the Civil War. The craftsmen in this movement worked primarily with hand tools, emulated medieval woodworkers, and even lived in communes similar to medieval craft guilds. The Arts and Crafts style emphasized simple, utilitarian designs, restrained decoration, and honest craftsmanship. This last characteristic often translated to exposed joinery (perhaps to show the client that the parts really were assembled with handmade joints). In America, Arts and Crafts pieces were referred to as *Mission* furniture, since the proponents were said to have a mission — a return to simpler designs and means of production. Craftsmen rejected the use of exotic woods or veneers; they worked mostly oak, because that was the choice of medieval woodworkers, but many Mission pieces were built from mahogany.

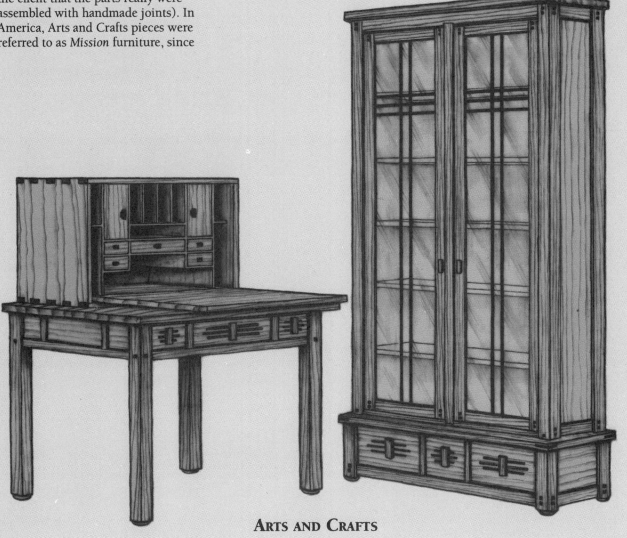

ARTS AND CRAFTS

(continued) ▷

DESK AND BOOKCASE STYLES — CONTINUED

7 **The Spanish conquerors** brought with them to America a furniture style that combined European furniture traditions with the *mujedar* — the decorative arts of the Moors. (The Moors were Moslems from North Africa who ruled Spain during the Dark Ages.) As part of the Spanish missionary efforts, immigrating craftsmen taught the enslaved Indians to reproduce Spanish furniture. The Indians found that the geometric designs of the *mujedar* were similar to their own and mixed the two, producing the *Southwest* style. This style, which survives today in Mexico and the western United States, uses simple forms decorated with intricate, geometric fretwork, turned spindles, and bright colors. Traditional Southwest furniture is made from native ponderosa pine, although today's Southwest craftsmen often import other woods.

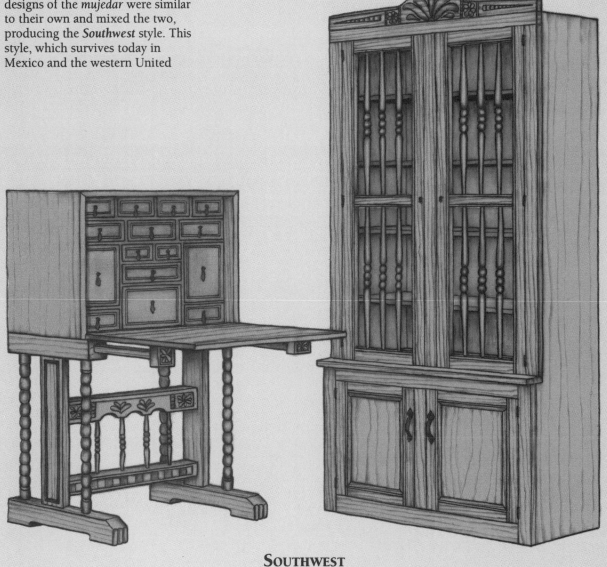

SOUTHWEST

8 **In America, the term** *contemporary* describes simple, elegant, lightweight furniture built in the second half of the twentieth century. The defining characteristic of contemporary American furniture is that it is purely functional with absolutely no decorative elements other than the form of the piece itself. The construction is as economical as possible. For example, contemporary bookcases have no face frames — the doors are hung on the sides of the case. Among contemporary craftsmen, the favorite woods are light, close-grained species such as maple and birch. Plywood, particleboard, metals, and plastics are also used freely.

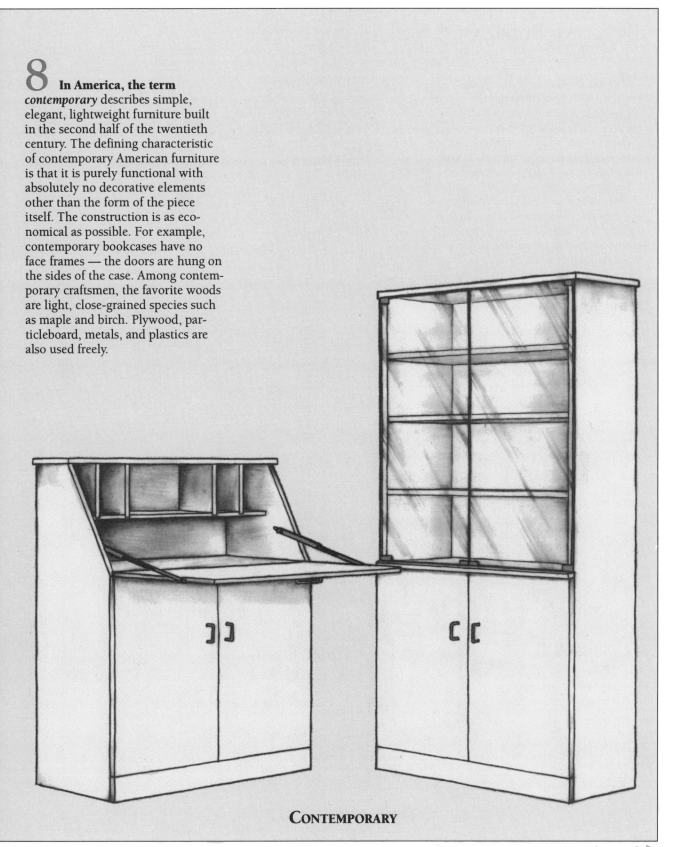

CONTEMPORARY

(continued) ▷

DESK AND BOOKCASE STYLES — CONTINUED

9 **Art dealers and critics use** the term *Handicraft Revival* to encompass the multitude of highly individual, imaginative furniture styles that are being built by craftsmen today. There is no central theme or definitive look to this furniture other than it is all handmade. Some craftsmen draw on historical designs for inspiration; others simply delight in their own ideas. Many designs are best described as whimsical. If there is any emphasis at all, it's on *technique*. Handicraft Revival craftsmen have invented many new woodworking methods and have pushed traditional techniques to new frontiers.

HANDICRAFT REVIVAL

2

BUILDING BOOKCASES

Bookcases come plain and fancy, in both appearance and method of construction. A small bookcase may be constructed like a simple bench; larger ones require more complex joinery. Traditional bookcases are usually built from solid wood with permanent joints; modern designs tend to be made from plywood and particleboard, and they often employ knock-down hardware. Many styles include shaped moldings and other decorative parts.

There is some common ground, however. All bookcases have at least two features in common — one or more horizontal shelves and vertical supports for these shelves. Furthermore, all bookcases are designed and built for storage. They must hold and display books or other objects within an arm's reach. No matter what type, style, or method of construction, the criteria for building a good bookcase remain the same.

MAKING THE CASE

CONSTRUCTION METHODS

There are three common ways to build a bookcase, depending on the type of case or framework.

The simplest of the three is the *rack* (hanging) or *bench* (standing) bookcase. It consists of just two or more shelves, vertical supports, minimal brace work, and little else. It has no back, no face frame, and no doors. Because large pieces of furniture need to be sturdier, this sort of construction is usually limited to small and medium-size shelving units. The whale

shelves shown in *FIGURE 1-5* on page 5 are a good example of a rack structure. (*SEE FIGURE 2-1.*)

A *traditional bookcase* has at least two shelves (top and bottom), two sides, a face frame, and (usually) a back. The back adds stability to the piece, while the face frame provides a surface on which to mount doors. (*SEE FIGURE 2-2.*) The step-back cabinet shown in *FIGURE 1-4* on page 4 is made using traditional construction.

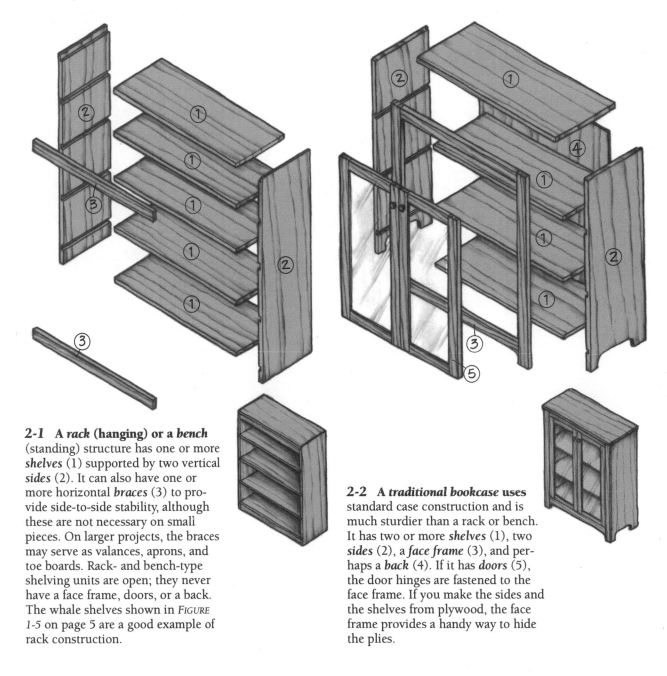

2-1 A *rack* (hanging) or a *bench* (standing) structure has one or more *shelves* (1) supported by two vertical *sides* (2). It can also have one or more horizontal *braces* (3) to provide side-to-side stability, although these are not necessary on small pieces. On larger projects, the braces may serve as valances, aprons, and toe boards. Rack- and bench-type shelving units are open; they never have a face frame, doors, or a back. The whale shelves shown in *FIGURE 1-5* on page 5 are a good example of rack construction.

2-2 A *traditional bookcase* uses standard case construction and is much sturdier than a rack or bench. It has two or more *shelves* (1), two *sides* (2), a *face frame* (3), and perhaps a *back* (4). If it has *doors* (5), the door hinges are fastened to the face frame. If you make the sides and the shelves from plywood, the face frame provides a handy way to hide the plies.

A *contemporary bookcase* differs from the traditional case in that it lacks a face frame and almost always has a back. In effect, it looks like a large box standing on one end. (*See Figure* 2-3.) The doors, if any, are hinged to the sides. The parts may be assembled with special hardware rather than with glued joints.

For Your Information

When the term *contemporary* describes furniture construction, it means something altogether different than when describing style. Contemporary furniture is highly functional with no unnecessary parts or ornament, as shown in "Desk and Bookcase Styles" on page 16. Contemporary *constructed* case furniture has no face frames and may use hardware in place of joinery. Contemporary construction is used to make contemporary style furniture, but you can also use it for other styles.

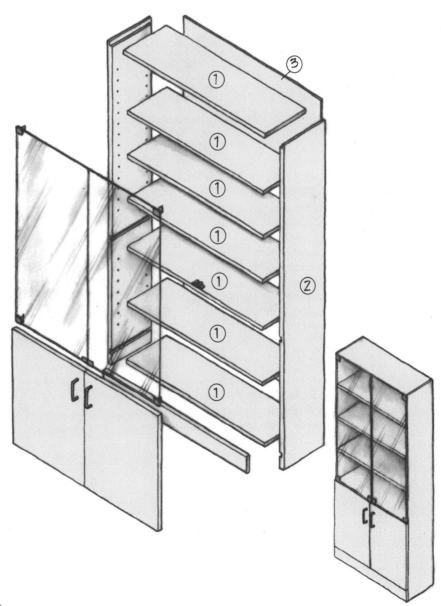

2-3 A *contemporary bookcase* has two or more *shelves* (1), two *sides* (2), and a *back* (3). There is no face frame; if the bookcase has doors, these are hinged directly to the sides. Often, contemporary-constructed furniture is made without traditional joinery and uses knock-down hardware instead. For more information on these special fittings, refer to "Knock-Down Hardware" on page 35.

In addition to these construction methods, you can build a bookcase with or without doors. *(See Figure 2-4.)* These doors are often *glazed* — that is, they have glass panels. But you can make them with solid (all wood) doors as well. Many large standing cases have glazed doors in the upper portion and solid doors in the lower part. *(See Figure 2-5.)*

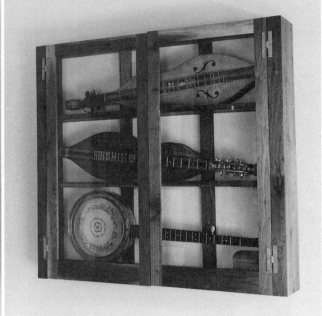

2-4 A shelving unit without doors is referred to as *open* shelves, while one with doors is *enclosed*. The Southwest-style hanging shelves shown are an open rack, while the contemporary hanging display case is an enclosed case. The objects in the display case are completely enclosed by wood and glass, while those on the hanging shelves are out in the open.

2-5 This large enclosed case has two different types of doors. The shelves in the lower portion are covered by *solid* doors, while those in the upper portion are covered by *glazed* doors — wood frames with glass panels. **Note:** The terms *cupboard* and *cabinet* were once used to designate the type of door that enclosed a space. The lower portion of this piece, which is enclosed by solid doors, is a cupboard space; the upper portion, with its glazed doors, is a cabinet. Today, the terms are often used interchangeably.

STANDARD DIMENSIONS

You can build a bookcase almost any size, depending on the space you have for the case and what you want to store in it. There are, however, several standards to help determine the height, width, depth, and level of shelves. You don't have to adhere to these, but you can use them as a starting point in planning your bookcase. (*SEE FIGURE 2-6.*)

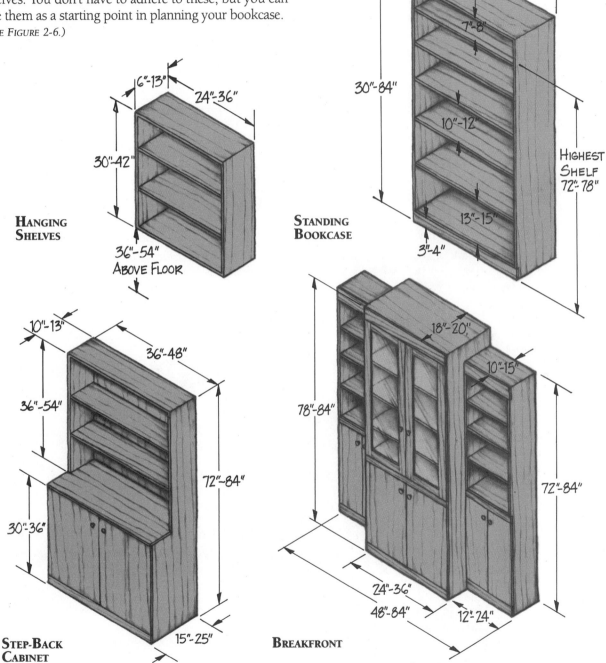

2-6 You can make a bookcase or set of shelves any size that you need. There are, however, *standard* sizes for various shelving units — ranges of dimensions to help determine the height, width, and depth of the piece, as well as the level and spacing of the shelves. Shown are the standard sizes for four common types of shelving units — hanging shelves, standing bookcase, step-back cabinet, and breakfront.

Height — You can build a bookcase to reach the ceiling if you want to use all the available space, but you might need a step stool to reach the highest shelves. Generally, bookcases are no higher than 84 inches so you can easily reach all the shelves. Small standing bookcases can be as low as 30 inches tall, and hanging bookcases are usually between 30 and 42 inches tall, if the bottom shelf is hung between waist and chest level (36 to 54 inches above the floor). A small rack or a single hanging shelf may be even shorter; a case hung with its bottom shelf below waist level may be taller.

Width — Just as you can build a bookcase as tall as you please, you can also make it any width. You can even fill an entire wall if you wish. Practically, however, the width between the sides of a bookcase is limited to between 24 and 60 inches. Any wider than this and the shelves may start to sag. (Refer to "Preventing Sagging Shelves" below.) If you need to make a wider case, add additional vertical supports or dividers between the sides.

Depth — The depth of a bookcase is determined by what you want to store in it. Most shelves will be between 6 and 25 inches deep, but you can make them deeper or shallower for special items:

- Small or narrow objects — 6 to 8 inches deep
- Books or large objects — 10 to 12 inches deep
- Kitchen items (above counter) — 12 to 13 inches deep
- Linens, clothes — 15 to 18 inches deep

PREVENTING SAGGING SHELVES

One of the most important dimensions in any bookcase project is the span of the shelves — the distance between the sides, dividers, or other vertical supports. If you make the span too long, the shelves will sag noticeably. How long is too long? That depends on four factors:

- The load the shelves must support
- The material the shelves are made from
- How and where the shelves are supported
- How the shelves are reinforced

1 **If you are unsure whether or not a shelving material will bridge a** span without sagging, perform this simple test. Make a single shelf, cutting it a few inches longer than the span. Place two blocks on your workbench so the distance between them is equal to the span. Rest the shelf across the blocks and weight it down with books or bricks to simulate the maximum load the shelf should support. **Note:** Ordinary construction bricks normally weigh about 2½ pounds apiece. Measure the distance of the shelf above the workbench at the blocks and halfway between them — the difference between the two is the amount of sag. If the shelf sags any more than 1/32 inch per foot, you must reduce the span, use a different shelving material, or reinforce the shelves.

- Audio components — 18 to 20 inches deep
- Video components — 18 to 24 inches deep
- Kitchen items (below counter) — 24 to 25 inches deep

Level of shelves — Generally, the highest shelf in a bookcase should be as high as you can comfortably reach. If the shelves are designed to be reached from a standing position, this is between 72 and 78 inches above the floor for most people. If you plan to reach the shelves from a seated position — sitting at your desk, perhaps — the highest shelf should be no more than 58 to 60 inches above the floor. The lowest shelf should be between 3 and 4 inches above the floor, not only to make the objects easier to reach, but to prevent you from accidentally kicking them or knocking them

over when you sweep. The space between shelves is determined by what you plan to keep on them. Generally, the shelves should be spaced 7 to 15 inches apart:

- Small objects and paperbacks — 7 to 8 inches apart
- Medium-size objects and hardcover books — 10 to 12 inches apart
- Large objects and tall books — 13 to 15 inches apart

In addition, the larger spaces should be located at the bottom of the bookcase and the smaller ones near the top. Otherwise, the case will look top-heavy. Of course, you can avoid the problem of shelf levels and spacing altogether by making *adjustable* shelves.

Most bookcase shelves must support 20 to 25 pounds per running foot. A 36-inch-long shelf, for example, must support up to 75 pounds without sagging noticeably — that is, more than $1/32$ inch per foot. This would mean a 36-inch-long shelf

shouldn't sag more than $3/32$ inch. To prevent or correct sagging shelves, you have three options:

- Use a different shelving material.
- Add vertical supports, reducing the span.
- Reinforce the shelving material.

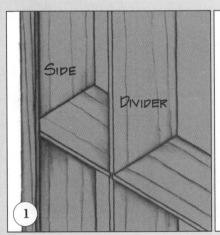

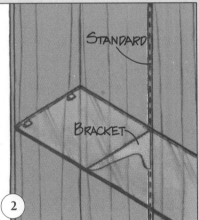

2 **The easiest way to reduce** the span is to make the bookcase narrower. If you'd rather not do this, there are other ways to add additional vertical support. Add dividers between the sides of the bookcase to break up the span (1). Use either braces or standards and brackets mounted to the back of the bookcase to support the shelves in the middle of the span (2). Add middle stiles to the face frame. If the shelves are fixed, attach the shelves to these stiles. If they are adjustable, mount shelving supports in the inside face of the stiles (3).

(continued) ▷

PREVENTING SAGGING SHELVES — CONTINUED

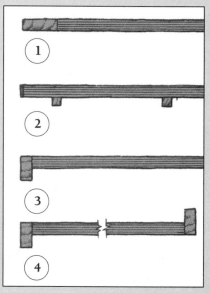

3 **If you can't reduce the** span, consider changing the shelving material. Particleboard (1) sags the most over a given span, followed by plywood (2). Solid wood (3) sags the least. Furthermore, the thicker the shelf material, the less it sags.

Note: *Stair treads,* which are sold at most building-supply centers, make strong, solid wood shelves. They are already sized to support hundreds of pounds — 1 inch by 10 inches by 36 inches, approximately.

4 **If you can't change the span** or the shelving material, there are several different ways to reinforce shelves to make them stronger. From the least to the most effective: Face the material with a solid strip of hardwood, glued edge to edge (1). Attach a strip of hardwood molding beneath the shelf (2). Cover the front edge with a strip of hardwood glued face to edge (3). Face *both* edges with strips of hardwood glued face to edge; arrange the back strip so it serves as a backstop (4).

MAXIMUM SHELVING SPANS (FOR 10-INCH-WIDE SHELVES SUPPORTING 20 POUNDS PER FOOT)

MATERIAL	MAXIMUM SPAN	MATERIAL	MAXIMUM SPAN
3/4" Particleboard	24"	3/4" Plywood, reinforced with a 3/4" x 1 1/2" oak strip glued edge to edge	33"
3/4" Plywood	30"		
3/4" Yellow pine	36"	3/4" Plywood, reinforced with two 3/4" x 3/4" oak strips glued to the bottom face	42"
1" Yellow pine	48"		
1 1/2" Yellow pine	66"	3/4" Plywood, reinforced with a 3/4" x 1 1/2" oak strip glued face to edge	42"
3/4" Oak	48"		
1" Oak	54"	3/4" Plywood, reinforced with two 3/4" x 1 1/2" oak strips glued face to edge	48"
1 1/2" Oak	78"		

BUILDING BOOKCASES FOR ELECTRONICS

When building shelving units for audio, video, and computer components, you face two special challenges. First, electronics generate heat that can build up in an *enclosed* case and harm the equipment or shorten its useful life. To prevent this, you must *ventilate* the enclosures to exhaust the heat. Second, you have to provide electrical power for each component and organize the power cords, patch cords, cables, and other wires to avoid a dangerous tangle.

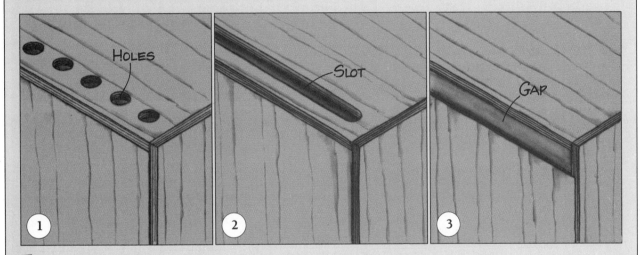

1   **When designing a ventilated** bookcase, remember that heat rises. The best place to exhaust the hot air is at the top of the case. There are three easy ways to do this. Drill a row or two of 1-inch-diameter holes in the top, near the back edge (1). Cut a 1-inch-wide slot in the top, near the back edge (2). Make the back slightly shorter than you would otherwise, and mount it to leave a 1-inch-wide gap at the top (3).
Warning: If you plan to operate the electronics with the doors closed, you must make an equal number of ventilation holes, slots, or gaps in the *bottom* of the case to draw cool air into it.

2   **You must not only exhaust** hot air from the top of the cabinet and draw it into the bottom but also allow the air to rise past the shelves. To do this, drill 1-inch-diameter holes near the back edge of each shelf (1), or cut each shelf 1 inch narrower than the depth of the case and fasten it to leave a 1-inch gap at the back (2).

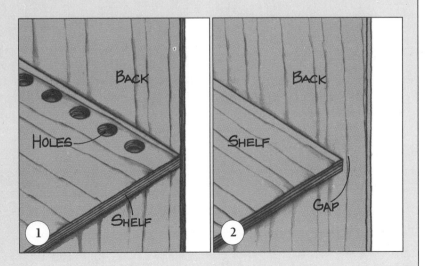

(continued) ▷

BUILDING BOOKCASES FOR ELECTRONICS — CONTINUED

3 **If you plan to store a lot of**
electronic components in a case or
if these components are particularly
sensitive to heat, you may not wish
to depend on passive ventilation.
Instead, mount one or two small *muffin fans* in the back of the bookcase,
near the top. (You may still have to
cut ventilation holes in the case
bottom.) These fans are very quiet.
They can be wired to operate when
you turn on the electronics or when
heat sensors are triggered by rising
temperatures inside the case. Muffin
fans and heat sensors are available at
most electronics-supply stores.

4 **The easiest way to provide**
power for all the electronic components is to mount a *plug strip* inside
the case and run the power cords to
it. That way, you'll only have one
power cord coming out of the case.
Make sure the plug strip has a built-
in circuit breaker to prevent an electrical overload. Some electronics —
particularly computer components —
also require a surge protector to
prevent damage from lightning
strikes and other sudden spikes in
the current. Locate the power strip
where you can reach it easily so you
can use the switch to turn all of the
components on and off at once.

(continued) ▷

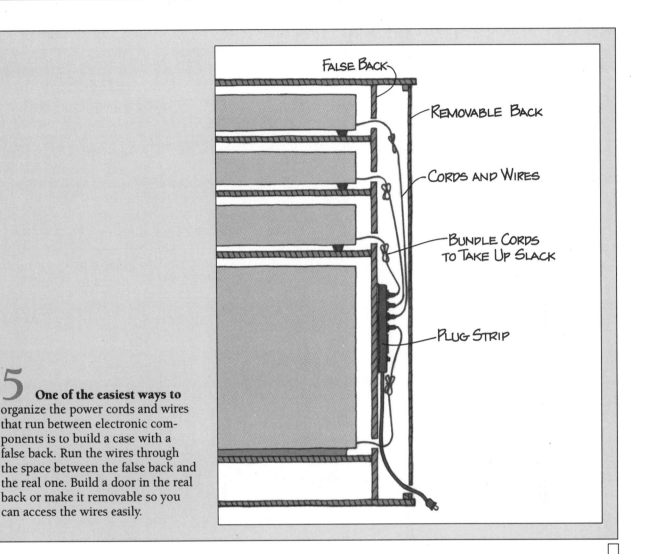

FALSE BACK

REMOVABLE BACK

CORDS AND WIRES

BUNDLE CORDS
TO TAKE UP SLACK

PLUG STRIP

5 **One of the easiest ways to** organize the power cords and wires that run between electronic components is to build a case with a false back. Run the wires through the space between the false back and the real one. Build a door in the real back or make it removable so you can access the wires easily.

KNOCK-DOWN HARDWARE

Contemporary furniture, especially pieces made from plywood and particleboard, often use knock-down fittings in place of permanent joinery. The reasons for this aren't just that these pieces are made to be easily assembled and disassembled. Knock-down hardware also often holds better in plywood and particleboard than glues, screws, nails, and other traditional fasteners that were designed for solid wood.

Knock-down hardware can be divided into two types — *inset* and *surface mounted*. Inset fasteners are hidden in the plywood or particleboard; surface-mounted fittings are attached to the surface.

Most inset hardware is designed to be installed with a hand drill or a drill press, while the surface-mounted variety often requires only a screwdriver. Use surface-mounted hardware when you can hide it beneath a shelf or inside a case, and use inset hardware when you need all sides of a bookcase to look good.

The chart on the following pages shows some of the more common knock-down hardware and their applications. Certain fittings, such as bed rail fasteners and corner brackets, are more often found on other types of furniture, but they can be used to assemble cases as well. All are available from mail-order woodworking suppliers.

(continued) ▷

KNOCK-DOWN HARDWARE AND APPLICATIONS

INSET HARDWARE

TYPE OF FITTING		APPLICATION
CONNECTOR BOLTS AND CAP NUTS 	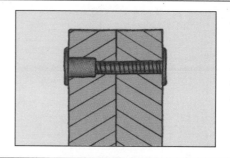	Joining small parts, joining large parts face to face, joining two cases side by side. Bolt heads and nuts are visible after assembly.
POSTS AND SCREWS 	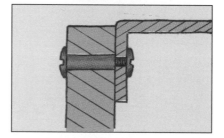	Similar to connector bolts and cap nuts, but suitable for small projects and light duty only.
CONNECTOR BOLTS AND BARREL NUTS 	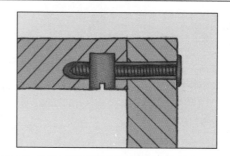	Joining face to edge, assembling corners, attaching dividers. Bolt heads are visible after assembly.
JOINT CONNECTORS 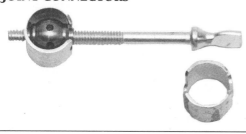	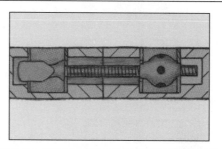	Joining edge to edge, assembling sections of large countertops.
BLUM FITTINGS 	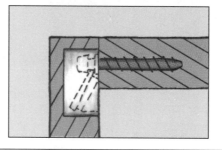	Joining face to edge, assembling corners, attaching dividers. When installed, these are almost completely hidden from view.

INSET HARDWARE

TYPE OF FITTING		APPLICATION
MINIFIX FITTINGS	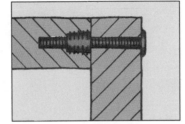	Similar to Blum fittings. They can also be hidden, though not as completely as Blum fittings.
THREADED INSERTS AND MACHINE SCREWS 	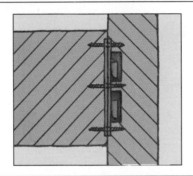	Joining small parts face to face and face to edge; light to medium duty.
BED RAIL FASTENERS 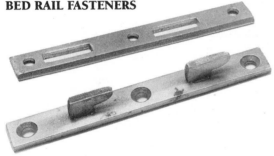	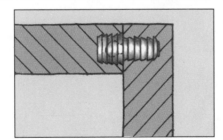	Assembling rails to posts.
INSET SNAP-TOGETHER FITTINGS	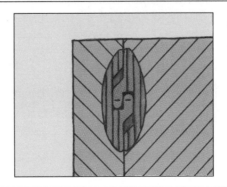	Applying panels and joining small parts; extremely light duty.
KNOCK-APART BISCUITS 		Joining small parts; light duty. Installed with a biscuit joiner.

(continued) ▷

KNOCK-DOWN HARDWARE AND APPLICATIONS — CONTINUED

SURFACE-MOUNTED HARDWARE

TYPE OF FITTING		APPLICATION
CORNER BRACES AND HANGER BOLTS 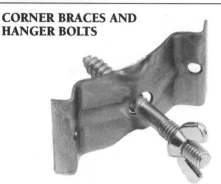	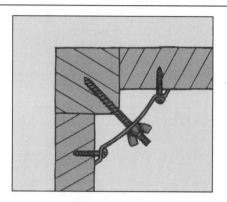	Attaching legs to aprons, attaching panels to posts.
SLIDE-TOGETHER FITTINGS 	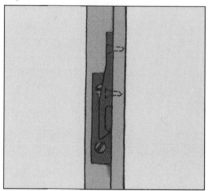	Attaching panels and frames, assembling rails to posts; light to medium duty.
LOCKING SLIDE-TOGETHER FITTINGS  	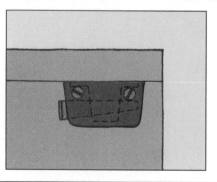	Joining face to edge, assembling corners, attaching dividers.
SURFACE SNAP-TOGETHER FITTINGS 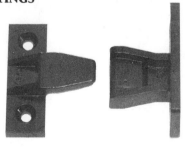	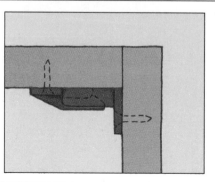	Attaching panels and frames; light duty.

SURFACE-MOUNTED HARDWARE

TYPE OF FITTING		APPLICATION
SCREW BLOCKS 	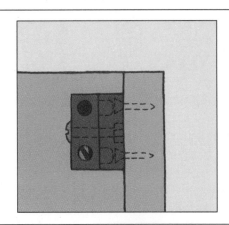	Joining face to edge, assembling corners, attaching dividers.
TAPER CONNECTORS 	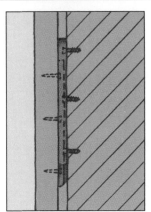	Joining face to face and face to edge, hanging shelves and cabinets. Although these fittings are surface mounted, they can be completely hidden after assembly.
SLIDE-ON CONNECTORS  	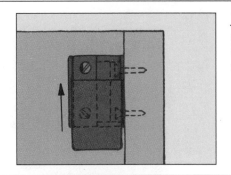	Joining face to edge, assembling corners, attaching dividers; light to medium duty.
FLUSH MOUNTS  	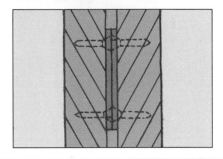	Joining face to face, attaching panels and frames, hanging shelves and cabinets.

3

INSTALLING SHELVES AND DOORS

You can install shelves and doors in a bookcase in a variety of ways. Attach the shelves permanently to the case sides with a variety of wood joints and hardware, or lay them across movable supports. Enclose the shelves with your choice of several doors, and hang them on any one of many hinges.

In short, you have a lot of choices. Your choice will depend on the type and style of the project, the tools and time available, and your personal tastes and needs.

INSTALLING SHELVES

You have two types of shelves to choose from. *Fixed* shelves are permanently attached to the bookcase sides or other vertical supports. *Adjustable* shelves remain movable so you can adapt their spacing as your storage needs change.

ATTACHING FIXED SHELVES

You can use either traditional wood joints or knockdown hardware to attach fixed shelves to a case. (*SEE FIGURE 3-1*.) Listed here are a few of the more common methods:

■ *Full dadoes* are perhaps the easiest way to install fixed shelves. Cut or rout dadoes in the vertical supports to hold the ends of the shelves. (*SEE FIGURE 3-2*.)

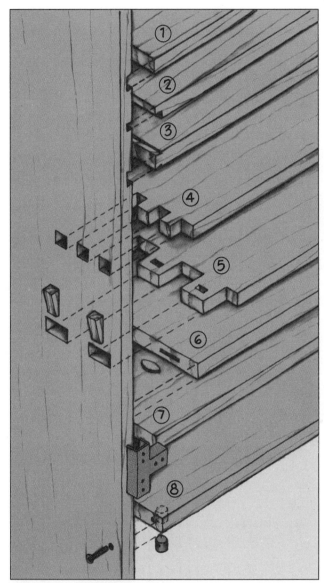

3-1 Some of the most common techniques for attaching fixed shelves in bookcases are *full dadoes* (1), *rabbet-and-dado joints* (2), *sliding dovetails* (3), *through mortise-and-tenon joints* (4), *keyed mortises and tenons* (5), *biscuits* (6), *metal shelving brackets* (7), and *connector bolts with barrel nuts* (8).

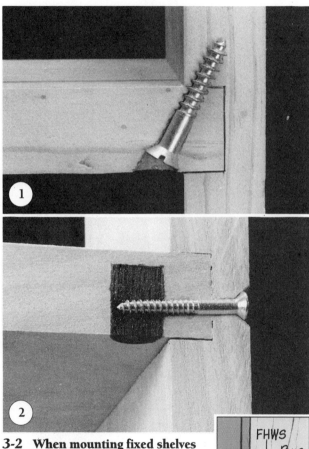

3-2 When mounting fixed shelves in full dadoes, it's often necessary to reinforce the joints with screws. You can drive the screws from the inside, angling them up through the shelf and into the side. This hides the screw heads (1). Or drive the screws from the outside of the case into the ends of the shelves, then hide the heads with plugs (2). However, screws don't hold particularly well in end grain. To make a stronger joint, install dowels near the ends of the shelves, as shown, and drive the screws through the dowels.

■ To make *rabbet-and-dado joints,* cut rabbets in the ends of the shelves to form tongues, then cut dadoes in the vertical supports to fit them. *(SEE FIGURE 3-3.)*

■ For *sliding dovetails,* cut or rout dovetail dadoes in the sides or supports, and make dovetail tenons to fit the dadoes. This joinery was used extensively in eighteenth- and early-nineteenth-century furniture styles, including Queen Anne and Federal designs. *(SEE FIGURE 3-4.)*

■ *Through mortises and tenons* are often made like finger joints when used to join shelves to a case. Cut several tenons, or fingers, in the ends of the shelves, then mortise the vertical supports to fit the fingers. *(SEE FIGURE 3-5.)*

■ *Keyed mortises and tenons* are made in the same way as ordinary mortise-and-tenon joints, but the tenons protrude through the vertical supports. The tenons themselves are mortised for wedge-shaped keys. When the keys are inserted through the tenons, they lock the shelves to the vertical supports. This joinery is most often used for knock-down shelving units. *(SEE FIGURE 3-6.)*

■ *Biscuits* require a biscuit or plate joiner. Use this power tool to cut semicircular slots in the ends of the shelves and faces of the vertical supports. Spread glue in the slots, insert the biscuits, and assemble the parts. *(SEE FIGURE 3-7.)*

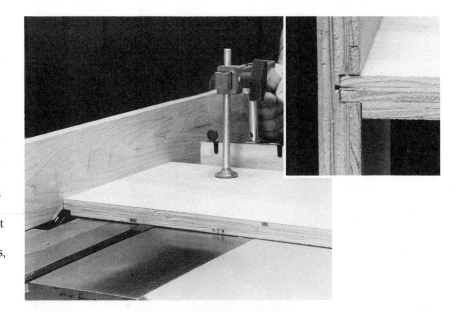

3-3 Rabbet-and-dado joints are slightly stronger than full dadoes because the rabbet forms a shoulder and prevents racking. These joints offer an additional advantage when working with plywood, which is usually $^1/_{32}$ inch smaller than its nominal size. Cabinet-grade $^3/_4$-inch plywood, for example, is really $^{23}/_{32}$ inch thick. This makes it difficult to rout or cut a full dado to the proper width — you must make two passes with a router bit or shim a stacked dado cutter. It's much easier to adjust the depth of cut to make a $^7/_{32}$-inch-deep rabbet on the ends of the shelves, creating $^1/_2$-inch-thick tenons, then rout or cut $^1/_2$-inch-wide dadoes to fit them.

3-4 When making a sliding dovetail joint, use the same router bit to cut both the tenons and the dadoes. Rout the dadoes in the bookcase sides, using either a hand-held or table-mounted router. Cut the matching tenons on a table-mounted router, using a tall fence or a tenoning jig to hold the shelves on end. Pass each end of each shelf by the bit, routing one side. Turn the shelf face for face and rout the other side.

3-5 Making ordinary *square*
mortise-and-tenon joints for shelves
is fairly straightforward, although
time-consuming. You must cut multiple tenons on the ends of the shelves,
mark the tenon positions on the
bookcase sides, drill holes to remove
most of the waste, and square the
holes with a chisel. (Whew.) If you
have a tenon cutter, you can make
round mortises and tenons much
more quickly. Simply cut the tenons
with a drill press or a horizontal
boring machine, pare away the
scrap, and drill holes to fit them.

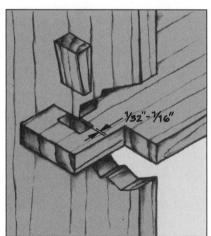

3-6 When making a keyed
mortise-and-tenon joint, the position
of the key mortise (the square hole
in the tenon that holds the key) is
critical. When the joint is assembled,
$1/32$ to $1/16$ inch of the key mortise
should be *inside* the larger mortise in
the side. When the key is tapped in
place, the shoulders of the tenon will
be drawn snug against the side. Also,
the tenon must be long enough to
keep from splitting out. If the key
mortise is too close to the end of the
tenon, the pressure from the wedge
will split the wood. To help prevent
the tenon from splitting out, you
might drive dowels through it, as
shown.

3-7 When using biscuits to join
shelves to the sides of a bookcase,
mark the positions of the biscuits
on all parts. Use the biscuit joiner's
fence to guide the tool when cutting
the slots in the ends of the shelves.
When cutting the slots in the sides,
remove the fence and use a straight-
edge to help control and guide the
biscuit joiner.

■ *Shelving brackets* are metal gussets that hold the shelves and supports together — just slip them over the parts and nail or screw them in place. These specialized fasteners are made to fit standard ¾-inch plywood and particleboard and should be used for light-duty shelving only. (*SEE FIGURE 3-8.*)

■ To use *connector bolts and barrel nuts,* bore small horizontal holes through the vertical supports and into the ends of the shelves for the bolts, then drill larger vertical holes in the underside of the shelves for the nuts. Insert the nuts first, then drive the bolts through them. (*SEE FIGURE 3-9.*)

VARIATIONS

Just because a shelf is fixed doesn't mean it can't be *movable.* Pull-out shelves make things more accessible and help you reach large or heavy objects. They are especially useful for storing televisions, amplifiers, printers, and other electronic equipment. You can purchase several types of extension slides for pull-out shelves, or you can make your own slides.

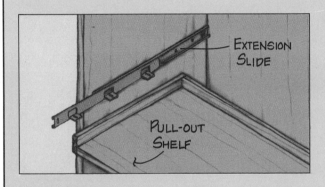

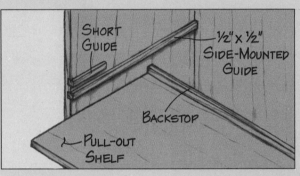

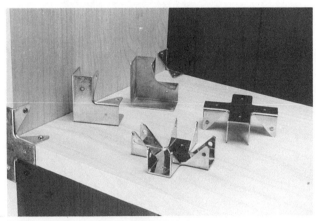

3-8 Metal brackets allow you to join plywood parts to make shelving units without cutting any joinery other than simple butt joints. They come in three shapes — L-shaped for assembling corners, T-shaped for attaching shelves or dividers, and cross-shaped for attaching shelves *and* dividers. Before putting the parts together, cover the plywood edges with banding, then sand and finish the individual pieces.

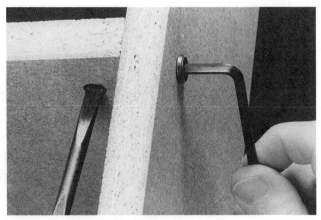

3-9 Connector bolts and barrel nuts make strong joints for bookcases made of plywood or particleboard — often much stronger than conventional joinery and fasteners. In addition, the parts can be easily disassembled, should you need to move or modify the shelving unit. **Note:** Drill the stopped holes for the barrel nuts in the *underside* of the shelves. This will help hide the nuts when the project is assembled.

INSTALLING ADJUSTABLE SHELVES

Oftentimes, only the top and bottom shelves in a bookcase are fixed, while those in the middle are adjustable.
This lets you adapt the bookcase to your changing
storage needs. Consider the variety of store-bought
hardware and shop-made movable supports:

■ *Shelving support pins* are perhaps the simplest
and easiest way to install adjustable shelving. Drill
rows of stopped holes in the sides of the bookcase to
hold the pins, spacing the holes evenly every 1 to 2
inches. You can purchase many styles of metal and
plastic pins, or you can make your own by cutting
short lengths of dowel stock. (*See Figures 3-10 and 3-11.*)

3-10 Shelving support pins range
from utilitarian to decorative. Most
are designed for wooden shelves; a
few are made for wood and glass.
These support pins usually fit in
¼-inch-diameter, ½-inch-deep
holes, although a few European
varieties require 5-millimeter holes.
You can also purchase metal bush-
ings, or *sockets,* to line the holes.
These sockets make the pins easier
to remove and replace, keep the pins
from wearing the holes, and add
decoration.

3-11 When using shelving support
pins, or any other type of shelving
hardware that must be mounted in
holes, it's essential that the rows of
holes be spaced precisely the same.
To help do this, make a drill guide
from a scrap of pegboard, as shown.
Attach cleats to one edge to help
align the pegboard, and mark the
holes you want to drill with paint
or gummed reinforcing rings. Also,
clearly mark the top and bottom of
the guide so you always orient it in
the same direction.

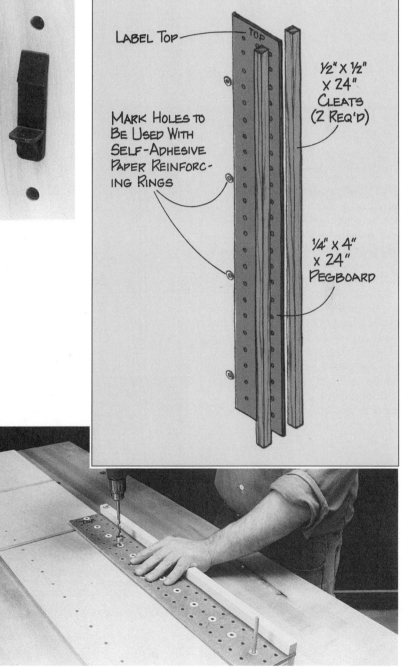

LABEL TOP

TOP

MARK HOLES TO
BE USED WITH
SELF-ADHESIVE
PAPER REINFORC-
ING RINGS

½" × ½"
× 24"
CLEATS
(2 REQ'D)

¼" × 4"
× 24"
PEGBOARD

■ To use *standards and brackets,* screw the metal standards to the bookcase sides or back, then insert the brackets in the standard slots. (*See Figures 3-12 and 3-13.*) You may wish to flush-mount the standards in grooves.

■ *Wire supports* fit into slots in the ends of the shelves, and are completely hidden when the shelves are installed. They cannot work loose, and they keep the shelves from tipping. (*See Figure 3-14.*)

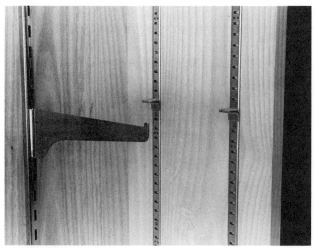

3-12 Side-mounted standards have horizontal slots and small brackets, or clips. **Back-mounted** or **wall-mounted** standards are somewhat larger and usually have vertical slots; the brackets are as long as the shelves are wide. Side-mounted standards are less obtrusive and can be almost completely hidden by the face frame of a bookcase. Back-mounted standards are better for wide shelving units or shelves that must support a heavy load. They can be mounted anywhere along the back of the case, and you can use as many as needed for proper support.

3-13 When mounting standards, take care to attach them all at the same level; otherwise, the shelves will tip. To do this, mount a bracket upside down in each standard, near the bottom end. Let this bracket rest against a spacer block as you attach the standards to the bookcase. Use the same spacer block for each standard.

3-14 To use wire supports, drill rows of evenly spaced stopped holes in the vertical supports, much like you would for support pins. Then cut horizontal slots in the ends of the shelves. Place the ends of the wire supports in the holes, and slide the slotted shelves over them. **Note:** Make the slots *blind* at the front edge of the shelf, or face the front edge with a strip of wood after cutting the slots. This way, you won't see the slots and the wire supports after installing the shelves.

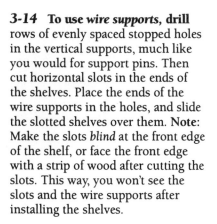

■ *Pins and slots* are one of the easiest systems you can make yourself. The shelves rest on wooden pins, and a combination of horizontal and vertical slots in the shelf ends keep them from tipping or sliding back and forth. (*See Figure 3-15.*)

■ *Cleats and notches* are another simple shop-made system — the ends of the wooden cleats fit notched supports. The cleat ends and matching notches can be any of several shapes — square, diamond, dovetail, or half-round. (*See Figure 3-16.*)

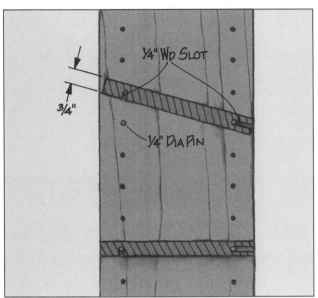

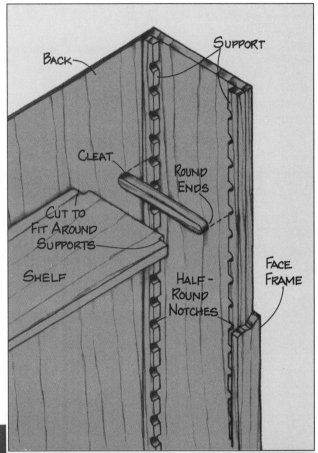

3-15 To make a *pin-and-slot* system, drill holes in the vertical supports and cut short lengths of dowels to make support pins. Then cut two blind slots in each end of each shelf — a *horizontal* slot near the back edge and a *vertical* slot near the front edge. To install the shelves, slip the back slots over the back pins, then let the front slots drop over the front pins.

3-16 To support adjustable shelves on movable *cleats* that rest in half-round *notches,* cut short strips of wood to make the cleats and longer strips for notched supports. Clamp each pair of supports together edge to edge and drill evenly spaced holes where the edges meet. The diameter of the holes must match the thickness of the cleats. When you remove the clamps and take the supports apart, the holes will split to form half-round notches. Attach these supports inside the bookcase. Round the ends of the cleats to fit the notches, and notch the ends of the shelves to fit between the supports.

■ You can make your own *wooden standards and brackets*. Design the brackets so they hang on the standards, or pin them in place with bolts or dowels. (SEE FIGURE 3-17.)

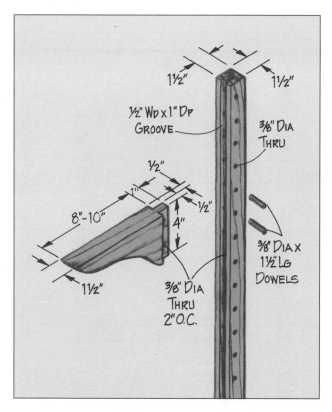

3-17   To make your own *wooden standards and brackets*, drill evenly spaced holes along the length of a wood strip. Cut a groove in the face of the strip to create a U-shaped channel. Cut the ends of the brackets to fit between the sides of the U, and drill holes in the brackets so you can pin them in place with dowels.

TRY THIS TRICK

Make your bookcase shelves with built-in *bookends*. Shown are several designs for sliding and clip-on bookends that can be adapted to both fixed and adjustable shelves.

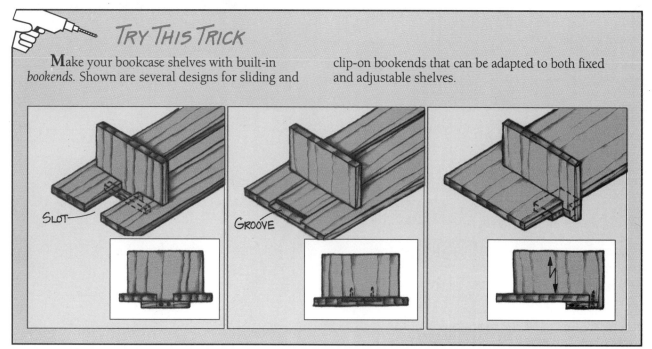

MAKING AND HANGING DOORS

DOOR TYPES AND SIZES

Four types of doors are commonly used to enclose bookcases (*SEE FIGURE 3-18*):

■ *Frame-and-panel* doors have a solid wood frame and a panel made from either wood or plywood. (*SEE FIGURE 3-19.*)

3-18 **There are four types of** doors commonly used in bookcases — *frame and panel* (1), *glazed* (2), *slab* (3), and *glass* (4). The type of door that looks best depends on the style of the bookcase. Frame-and-panel doors, for instance, work well on classic and traditional styles such as Queen Anne, Federal, country, Shaker, and Southwest. Glazed doors work well in most styles, including Queen Anne, Federal, Victorian Oak, and Arts and Crafts. Large plywood and particleboard slab doors are most commonly used for contemporary pieces, but small wooden slab doors are often employed in classic and traditional designs. Glass doors work best in contemporary and other modern designs.

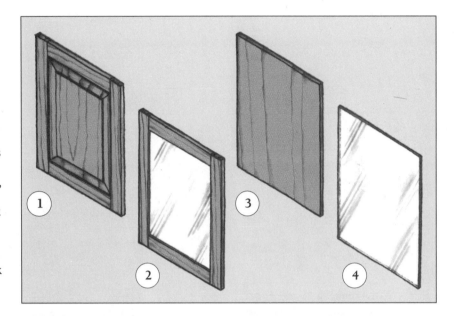

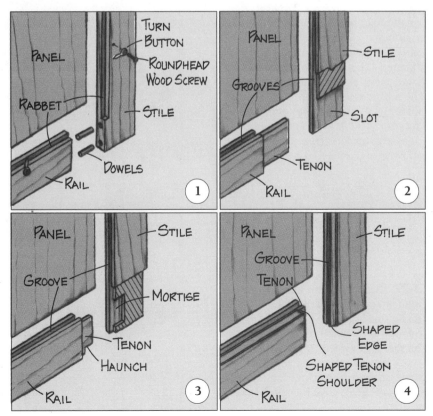

3-19 **A frame-and-panel door** consists of two vertical *stiles,* two horizontal *rails,* and a *panel.* The rails and stiles are joined to form a frame, while the panel rests in grooves in the inside edges of the frame members. Shown are four common ways to join the rails and stiles — *dowels* (1), *bridle joints* (2), *haunched mortises and tenons* (3), and shaped *sash joints* (4).

■ *Glazed* doors have a solid wood frame and a glass panel. Many glazed doors, particularly those on classic and traditional styles of furniture, have a delicate wooden framework called *sash work* inside a sturdy outside frame. This sash work holds several small glass panes. (*SEE FIGURE 3-20.*)

■ *Slab* doors are made from a single piece of wood, plywood, or particleboard. Usually, only small slab doors are made from solid wood; larger doors are made from manufactured materials to prevent cupping and warping. (*SEE FIGURE 3-21.*)

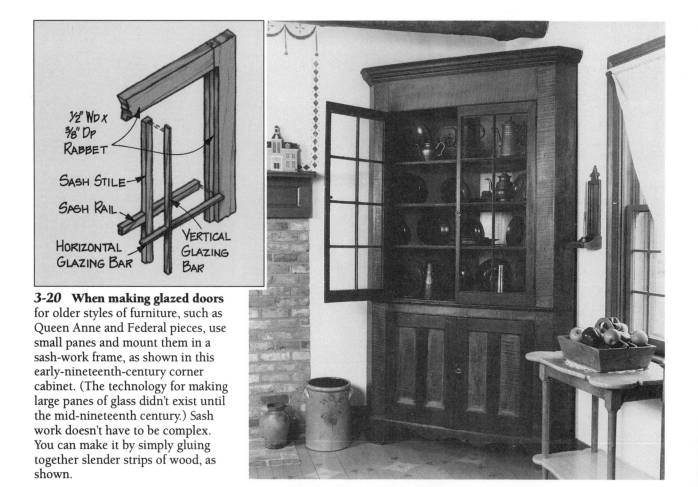

3-20 When making glazed doors for older styles of furniture, such as Queen Anne and Federal pieces, use small panes and mount them in a sash-work frame, as shown in this early-nineteenth-century corner cabinet. (The technology for making large panes of glass didn't exist until the mid-nineteenth century.) Sash work doesn't have to be complex. You can make it by simply gluing together slender strips of wood, as shown.

3-21 Because plain-sawn wood tends to cup and warp, it's best to make small wooden slab doors from quarter-sawn wood. If quarter-sawn lumber isn't available, rip plain-sawn stock into narrow strips and turn them so the annual rings run face to face, as shown. Glue the strips edge to edge.

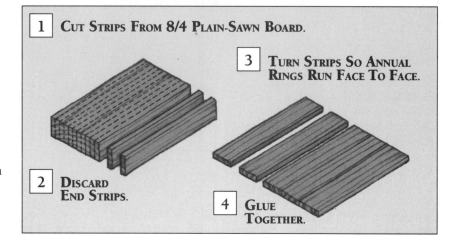

■ *Glass* doors are made of single sheets of tempered glass or other strong, transparent plastics. They have no frame and require special hardware to be hung in a bookcase. (*SEE FIGURE 3-22.*)

Before cutting or building a door, you must determine its overall size. This depends on not only the size of the door opening, but also on how the door covers the opening. It can be **inset** in the opening, it can **overlay** the opening, or it can be **lipped** so only the rabbeted lips overlay the opening. (*SEE FIGURE 3-23.*) **Note:** Glass doors are always inset.

An **inset** door is customarily sized $1/32$ to $1/16$ inch smaller than the door opening on all four sides. Many cabinetmakers prefer to build inset doors the same size as the opening, then trim them to fit.

TRY THIS TRICK

If the bookcase doors or door frames are made from solid wood, fit them loose in the winter (when the wood has shrunk) and tight in the summer (when the wood has expanded).

You determine the size of an *overlay* door by whether or not the bookcase has a face frame. If it has a face frame, the door normally overlaps it by $3/8$ inch. If it doesn't, the door covers the front edges of the case. Some edges may be entirely covered by one door — this is a *full overlay*. Others are covered half by one door and half by an adjoining door — this is a *half overlay*. The size of the door depends on which sides are full overlays, which sides are half overlays, and the clearance required between the adjoining doors.

A *lipped* door is customarily $5/16$ inch larger than the opening on each lipped side. The rabbets that create the lips are $3/8$ inch wide and $3/8$ inch deep, so there is a $1/16$-inch gap between the shoulder of each rabbet and the bookcase carcase.

3-22 Glass doors have no frame; they're single panes of glass that pivot on special hinges. For safety, use $1/4$-inch-thick *tempered* glass for this application — it's much stronger than ordinary glass. If the bookcase will be used by children, incredibly clumsy adults, people who toss horseshoes indoors, or even the horses themselves, use acrylic plastic instead.

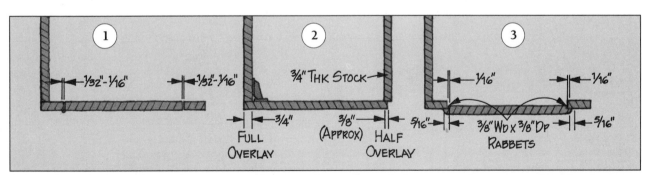

3-23 The size of a bookcase door depends on the size of the opening and how the door covers that opening. A door can be *inset* (1) in the opening; it can *overlay* (2) the opening; or it may be *lipped* (3), in the case of an inset door with overlaid lips. As a rule of thumb, older furniture styles — such as Queen Anne, Federal, country, and Shaker — use inset doors. Lipped doors have been in common use since the late nineteenth century, and overlay doors are most often found on contemporary pieces and other modern styles. However, there are many exceptions to these guidelines.

HANGING DOORS

To hang a door, first fit it to its opening. Using a hand plane, scraper, or sander, carefully shave the door's edges until it fits the case properly. When fitting a lipped door, use a bullnose plane or a rabbet plane to shave the shoulders of the rabbets. However, do *not* plane the rabbet on the side where you will install the hinges. If you change the dimensions of this lip, the hinges may not fit properly.

The method of hanging a door depends on the type of door and the hinges that you use. The three most commonly used hinges for wooden and wood-framed doors are **butt hinges, surface-mounted hinges,** and **concealed hinges.** When hanging glass doors, use **bracket hinges.**

Butt hinges are normally used to hang inset wooden and wood-framed doors and must be mortised into the bookcase and the door frame. (*See Figures 3-24 and 3-25.*) They are not well suited for slab doors made from plywood and particleboard — the screws tend to pull out. If you want the look of butt hinges and need to hang doors made from manufactured materials, use *wrap-around hinges.* (*See Figure 3-26.*)

Surface-mounted hinges are used to hang all three kinds of doors. They require no mortises. Instead, they are fastened directly to the bookcase and the door. There are many types of hinges for inset doors, both decorative and plain — H-hinges, butterfly hinges,

rat-tail hinges, strap hinges, and so on. To install these, simply wedge the door in place, and mount the hinges so they straddle the gap betweeen the door and the case. Surface-mounted hinges for lipped and overlay doors must be mounted to the door first, then the case. (*See Figures 3-27 and 3-28.*) **Note:** Hinges for lipped doors are often referred to as *offset hinges.*

Concealed hinges (also called *European-style hinges* and *Euro-hinges*) are specially designed for bookcases that have no face frames and will hang inset and overlay doors. Unlike many other types of hinges, these can be adjusted front to back, side to side, and up and down. This allows you to set the position of the door *after* it's installed. (*See Figures 3-29 through 3-31.*)

Bracket hinges cradle glass doors in metal brackets, holding them in place with pressure screws. These brackets are attached to pivots, and the pivots are mounted in the bookcase. (*See Figure 3-32.*)

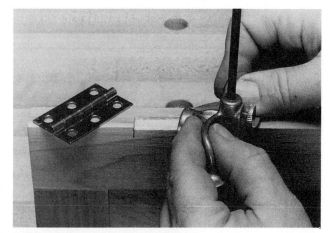

3-25 Cut mortises for the hinge leaves in the case and the door frame. Each mortise must be precisely the same depth as one leaf. Cut the perimeter of the mortises with a chisel, then cut the bottoms to a uniform depth using a router or router plane (shown). Drill pilot holes for the hinge screws in each of the mortises, install the hinges on the door, and hang the door on the bookcase. **Note:** If you need to adjust the hinge positions, remove the screws and fill the holes with toothpicks or matchsticks. If necessary, enlarge the mortises slightly. Then drive new pilot holes just to one side of the old ones.

3-24 To hang a bookcase door on butt hinges, first mark the location of the hinges on the case. Fit the door to the case and wedge it in place with slivers of wood or cardboard. Transfer the marks from the case to the door frame.

3-26 Because butt hinges are screwed into the edges of doors, the screws may not hold in plywood or particleboard. Instead, use *wrap-around hinges* for doors made from manufactured materials. These look like butt hinges when installed, but they wrap around the back of the door and are screwed to the inside face. Some also wrap around the back of the face frame.

3-27 To hang a lipped or overlaid bookcase door on surface-mounted hinges, first screw the large hinge leaves to the inside face of the door. You don't have to cut mortises to install these hinges. However, if you're using *offset* surface-mounted hinges, make sure the bend in each hinge leaf is snug against the shoulder of the rabbet.

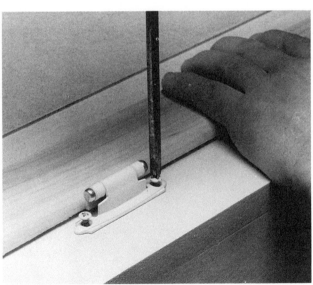

3-28 Clamp the door in place on the bookcase. The small hinge leaves should protrude from under one edge of the door. Screw these to the case and remove the clamps from the door. **Note:** If you need to adjust the hinge positions, follow the same procedure as for butt hinges — plug the old screw holes and drill new ones.

3-29 To hang a door on concealed hinges, take the hinges apart, separating the cups from the plates. Mark the locations of the hinge cups on the inside surface of the door. Drill a 1³⁄₈-inch-diameter, ¹⁄₂-inch-deep (135 millimeter by 13 millimeter) hole at each cup location. (Most concealed-hinge manufacturers offer special drill bits for this operation.) Insert the hinge cups in the holes and screw the flanges to the door.

3-30 Drill pilot holes inside the case to mount the hinge plates. (You can purchase templates to help locate these screw holes, or you can make your own from a scrap of plastic or plywood.) Screw the plates to the case.

3-31 With the hinge cups attached to the door and the plates mounted in the bookcase, slide the two parts together and tighten the locking screws. If necessary, use the adjusting screws to correct the position of the door. (Unlike most other types of hinges, you don't have to remove the screws and plug the holes to do this.)

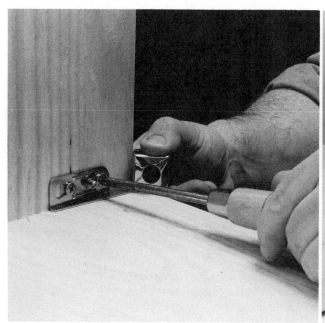

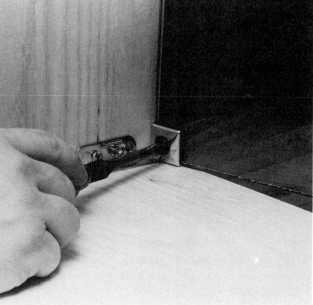

3-32 To mount a glass door on bracket hinges, first attach the hinges to the inside surfaces of the bookcase. Then slide the glass into the brackets and tighten the pressure screws. To adjust the position of the door, loosen the pressure screws, move the door in the brackets, and tighten the screws again.

4

BUILDING DESKS

The carcase of a desk is often more complex than that of a bookcase for the simple reason that it must do more. Both pieces provide storage space, but a desk also provides a place to work. The addition of the work surface, and the arrangement of the storage around it, make a desk a more challenging project to plan and build.

MAKING THE DESK CASE

DESK CONSTRUCTION METHODS

Like bookcases, case-constructed desks can be classi-fied as traditional or contemporary. However, because of the wide range of types, styles, and sizes, desks employ many other methods of construction besides case joinery.

As an example, a slant-front desk is built with ordi-nary *case construction*. Like a traditional bookcase, a desk case has two sides joined by shelves and other horizontal parts. A back provides stability and keeps the case square. *(SEE FIGURE 4-1.)* Fall-front desks, secretaries, and kneehole desks also rely on case joinery.

Small desks, such as lap desks and writing boxes, are usually built with simple *box construction*. The sides join the ends with dovetails, finger joints, or some other corner joint. The bottom is attached in such a way that it can *float* — expand and contract without stressing the corner joints. The lid also floats, since only one edge is hinged to the box. *(SEE FIGURE 4-2.)*

Table desks and writing tables use *leg-and-rail con-struction,* like a table or a chair. The writing surface is supported by legs and aprons. The desk box, if there is one, is either box constructed or case constructed and sits on top of the writing surface. *(SEE FIGURE 4-3.)*

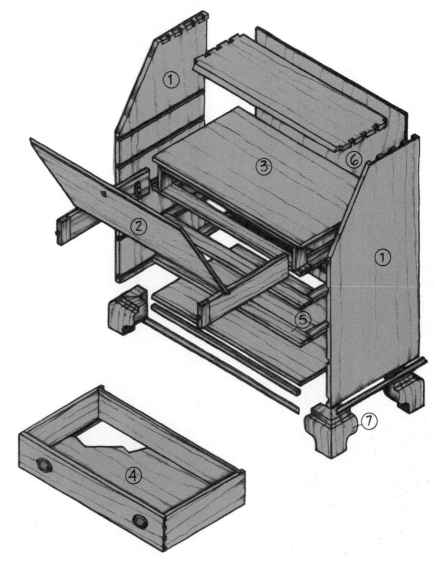

4-1 Slant-front desks and many other desk types are *case constructed.* A desk case has two vertical *sides* (1) joined by several horizontal parts such as the **work surface** (2) and **shelves** (3). If there are **drawers** (4) in the case, these are often supported by **web frames** (5). A **back** (6) pro-vides stability. Sometimes the case rests on **bracket feet** (7), although the feet may also be extensions of the sides.

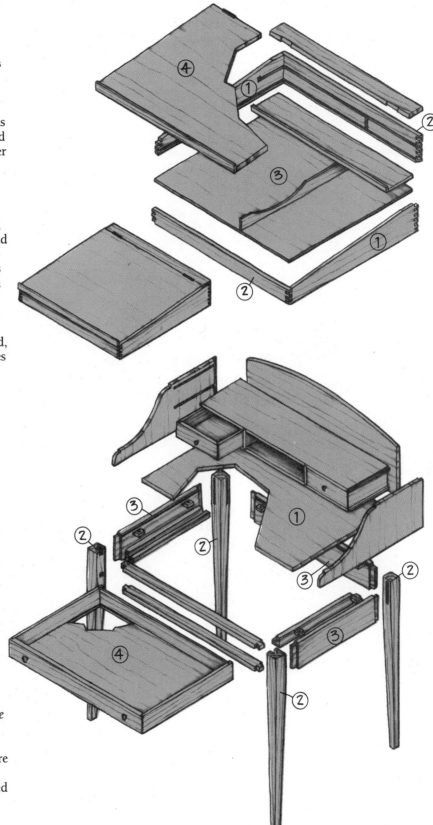

4-2 Lap desks and writing boxes are built using simple *box construction*. The *sides* (1) and *ends* (2) are joined to form a rectangle. The *bottom* (3) is attached to the other parts in such a way that it can expand and contract without stressing the corner joints. (In a writing desk, the box stands on a side or an end, opening from the front rather than from the top.) In some box assemblies, the bottom floats in a groove. In others, it's nailed or screwed to the sides and ends. Nails bend slightly as the bottom moves, and screws usually pass through slotted or enlarged holes in the bottom. The *lid* (4) also moves without constraint, since it's hinged to the assembly along one edge. **Note:** Although they don't have a lid, most desk drawers are also examples of box construction.

4-3 Table desks employ *leg-and-rail construction*. The *writing surface* (1) is supported by four *legs* (2). These legs are joined by rails, or *aprons,* (3) to provide stability. There may be one or more *drawers* (4) under the writing surface, suspended between the aprons. Other components of the desk sit on top of the writing surface.

Pedestal desks and rolltop desks are built using a combination of case joinery and *frame-and-panel construction*. Because the back and sides are so wide, these parts are finished frames with panels — wide

boards would expand and contract too much. The frames are joined to make two cases or pedestals, which support the work surface. (SEE FIGURE 4-4.)

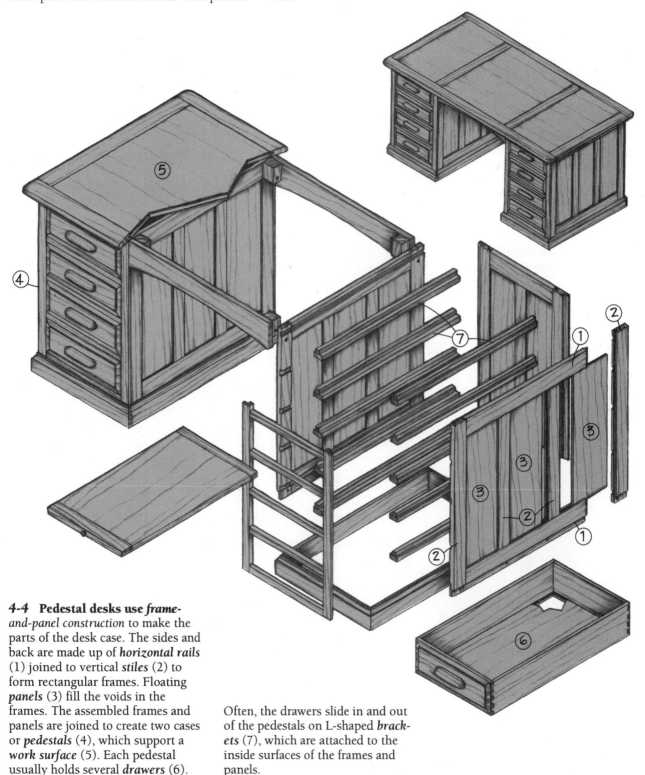

4-4 Pedestal desks use *frame-and-panel construction* to make the parts of the desk case. The sides and back are made up of *horizontal rails* (1) joined to vertical *stiles* (2) to form rectangular frames. Floating *panels* (3) fill the voids in the frames. The assembled frames and panels are joined to create two cases or *pedestals* (4), which support a *work surface* (5). Each pedestal usually holds several *drawers* (6).

Often, the drawers slide in and out of the pedestals on L-shaped *brackets* (7), which are attached to the inside surfaces of the frames and panels.

Contemporary and modern office furniture, such as computer desks, often employ *trestle construction* — the work surface is supported at the ends by two trestles. (This is very similar to bench-constructed bookcases.) These trestles may be solid wood frames or sheets of plywood or particleboard. Often, the trestles extend above the work surface to support shelves and cupboards. *(SEE FIGURE 4-5.)* **Note:** Although much modern furniture is trestle built, this isn't a new type of construction. The earliest tables rested on trestles, as does the old-time Southwest fall-front desk shown in "Desk and Bookcase Styles" on page 16. And campaign desks, the portable writing tables that were popular during the eighteenth and nineteenth centuries, rested on folding trestles.

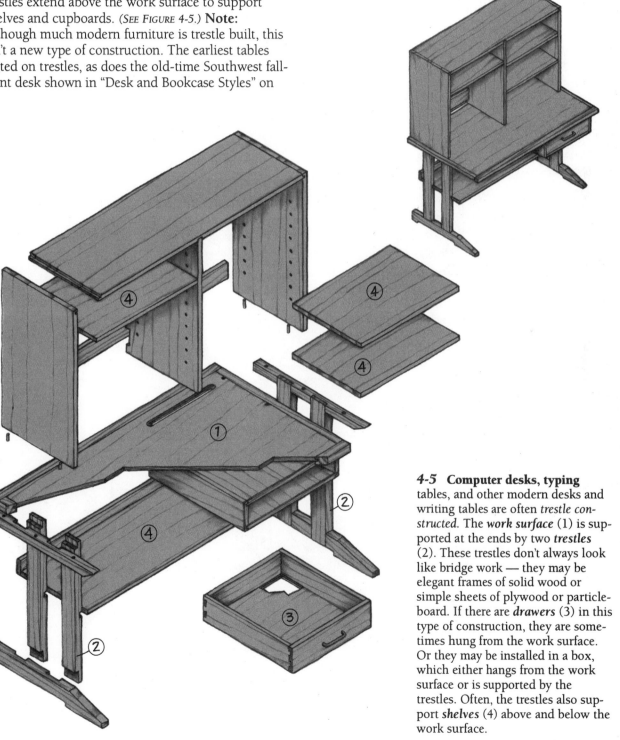

4-5 Computer desks, typing tables, and other modern desks and writing tables are often *trestle constructed*. The **work surface** (1) is supported at the ends by two **trestles** (2). These trestles don't always look like bridge work — they may be elegant frames of solid wood or simple sheets of plywood or particleboard. If there are **drawers** (3) in this type of construction, they are sometimes hung from the work surface. Or they may be installed in a box, which either hangs from the work surface or is supported by the trestles. Often, the trestles also support **shelves** (4) above and below the work surface.

DESK ERGONOMICS

Just as desk construction is more varied and complex than building a bookcase, so is figuring the dimensions of a desk. A desk can't simply be sized to hold objects; it must be tailored to allow a human being to work comfortably. The science of designing comfortable furniture is known as *ergonomics*.

Note: In the following discussion and the chart of "Standard Desk Dimensions" on the facing page, the term *depth* is used in two ways. When referring to drawers, it denotes a vertical measurement — the distance from the top of the drawer to the bottom. When describing work surfaces and knee spaces, and in all other instances, it signifies a horizontal measurement — the front-to-back distance as you sit at the desk.

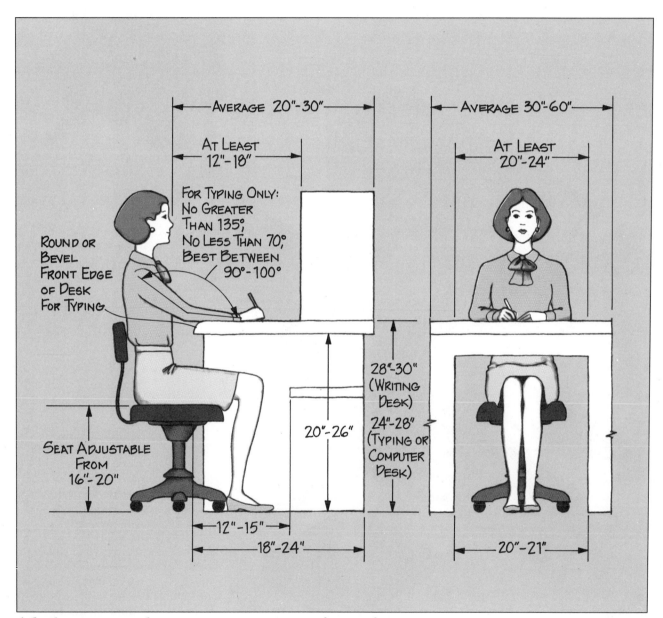

4-6 Shown are general measurements for a writing desk and a typing desk, built to fit most men and women. These numbers are suggestions, not laws. Use them as a starting point when you design a desk, but let your own size, work habits, and preferences determine the most comfortable dimensions for you.

FITTING THE DESK TO A PERSON

The first step in making an ergonomic desk is to fit it to the person who will use it. There is a range of important dimensions that are generally best for any well-designed desk, no matter what the type of style. (*SEE FIGURE 4-6.*)

Work surface — Perhaps the most important dimension is the height of the work surface. When seated, people usually prefer to work on a surface that's 28 to 30 inches above the floor — for *most* tasks. The important exception to this rule is typing, either on a typewriter or a computer keyboard. Typing is more comfortable when the work surface is 24 to 28 inches high — with your arms resting on the keyboard, the angle of your elbows should be no less than 70 degrees and no more than 135 degrees. Most people find an angle between 90 and 100 degrees to be the most comfortable. Furthermore, if you spend long periods of time at your keyboard, it helps to make the level of

STANDARD DESK DIMENSIONS

DESKS				
TYPE OF DESK	**WORK SURFACE HEIGHT**	**OVERALL HEIGHT**	**OVERALL WIDTH**	**OVERALL DEPTH**
Lap desk	4"–6"	4"–6"	20"–24"	12"–18"
Slant-front desk	28"–30"	40"–42"	36"–42"	18"–24"
Secretary	28"–30"	78"–84"	36"–42"	18"–24"
Writing table	28"–30"	28"–30"	36"–40"	20"–24"
Table desk	28"–30"	38"–68"	30"–48"	20"–30"
Pedestal desk	28"–30"	28"–30"	48"–72"	24"–30"
Rolltop desk	28"–30"	40"–48"	48"–72"	24"–30"
Typing table	24"–28"	24"–28"	36"–42"	16"–24"
Computer desk	24"–28"	24"–58"	24"–60"	20"–30"
Children's desk	20"–22"	20"–22"	24"–30"	18"–20"

DESK STORAGE				
COMPONENT	**HEIGHT**	**WIDTH**	**DEPTH**	**LENGTH**
Drawers*				
Above knee space	N/A	20"–24"	2"–4"	18"–28"
Beside knee space	N/A	12"–18"	4"–10"	18"–28"
Behind knee space	N/A	34"–40"	4"–10"	16"–22"
Letter file	N/A	12"†	10"	18"–28"
Legal file	N/A	15"†	10"	18"–28"
Compartments				
Envelope	4½"–7"	2"–3"	7"–10"	N/A
Stationery	1½"–2"	12"	7"–10"	N/A
Stamp drawer	1½"–3"	3½"–5"	7"–10"	N/A

*All drawer dimensions are inside measurements.
†For hanging files, add ½" to the width and 1" to the depth.

the work surface easily *adjustable* so you can change the height from time to time. This helps prevent back strain, wrist injuries, and general fatigue.

The width and depth of the work surface varies widely. Generally, the desk feels cramped if the actual working space is less than 20 to 24 inches wide and 12 to 18 inches deep (the size of a lap desk). On the other end of the scale, standing desks can be as large as you want to make them. Practically, however, it becomes difficult to reach the materials on the desk if the work surface is too large. For this reason, most standing desks are 30 to 60 inches wide and 20 to 30 inches deep.

FOR YOUR INFORMATION

An old school of thought says that desk work surfaces should be *slanted* toward the person sitting at them. When a work surface is flat, you have to constantly refocus your eyes to shift between things that are close and far away. On a slanted work surface, the objects are roughly in the same focal plane, and there is less strain on your eyes. This is the reason that drafting boards are angled. Unfortunately, it isn't practical for most general-purpose desks — objects tend to slide off a slanted surface. However, a few desk designs, like the table desk shown, include *both* flat and slanted surfaces. ·

Knee space — The space under the desk is just as important as the space on top of it. If the space for your legs is cramped, the desk won't be comfortable. Depending on the height and general build of the person using the desk, the knee space should be 20 to 26 inches tall and *at least* 20 to 24 inches wide. It must also be 12 to 15 inches deep so a person's knees don't bump the back of the desk. The *toe space* (under the knee space and closer to the floor) must be even deeper — roughly 18 to 24 inches — to prevent toes from bumping.

FOR YOUR INFORMATION

Designing a comfortable desk is only half the battle — you must also find a comfortable desk chair. Most people prefer a chair with a seat 16 to 17 inches high. However, if you sit at your desk for long periods, purchase a chair that can be easily adjusted from 16 to 20 inches. This will allow you to change the seat level from time to time to help prevent fatigue.

DESK STORAGE SPACES

Once you've tailored the desk to a human being, you can begin to fill the spaces in the desk with drawers and compartments to hold files, stationery, pencils, and other materials needed for desk-bound activities.

Drawers — The drawers in a desk can be almost any size, but there are some rules of thumb that govern their dimensions. Perhaps the most obvious is that the drawers installed under the work surface are generally much larger than those installed above it. The upper drawers store small office supplies, such as paper clips and stamps, and can be made almost as small as you like — provided you can still reach into them easily.

The lower drawers hold larger items or more of them. These drawers can be (and usually are) as long as the desk is deep. They shouldn't be much narrower than 12 inches (inside dimension) so they will hold a standard piece of paper lengthwise. A drawer over the knee space must be kept shallow — sometimes just 2 or 3 inches deep — since there's not much room between your knees and the work surface. The drawers to either side of the knee space (as in a pedestal desk) or in back of the knee space (as in a slant-front desk with the work surface folded out) are between 4 and 10 inches deep. Place the deeper drawers toward the bottom of the case and the shallower drawers toward the top; this arrangement will look better.

The only desk drawers that must be sized precisely are *file drawers*. These should be 10 inches deep. If meant to hold letter files, they should be 12 inches wide; for legal files, 15 inches wide. If you want to put a hanger frame inside the drawer for hanging letter files, make the drawer 11 inches deep and 12½ inches wide; for hanging legal files, 11 inches deep and 15½ inches wide. **Note:** All these numbers are *inside* dimensions.

Compartments — Many types of desks, such as slant-front desks and rolltops, have multiple compartments, or pigeonholes, above the work surface. Set these assemblies toward the back of the work surface, leaving at least 12 to 18 inches of clear space in front of them. Although it can be any size you want it to be, a pigeonhole assembly is usually no more than 12 to 14 inches tall and 7 to 10 inches deep. It often stretches the entire width of the desk. The size of the individual compartments depends on their use. If a compartment is intended to organize bills and envelopes, it should be 2 to 3 inches wide and at least 4½ inches tall. Stationery compartments must be 12 inches wide and are only 1½ to 2 inches tall. A compartment housing a small drawer may be only 1½ inches deep and 3 inches wide.

DESIGNING A COMPUTER WORKSTATION

Few inventions have had as big an impact on office furniture as the personal computer. The filing system and the typewriter merited their own pieces of furniture, but a filing cabinet and a typing table are simply reincarnations of older forms (the chest of drawers and the writing table). The computer, however, initiated a whole new wrinkle in desk design — the *workstation*. The purpose of the computer workstation is to hold all the computer components — central processing unit (CPU), disk drives, keyboard, monitor, printer, and mouse — in the proper relationship to each other and the computer operator.

CPU — In some ways, the placement of the CPU is the least of your concerns when designing a workstation. You must be able to reach the on/off switch, the reset button, and the disk drives (if the drives are mounted in the CPU box), but you can put the CPU almost anywhere within an arm's length. Your only constraint is that this box must be central to the other components, so all the connecting cables will reach.

Many operators place the CPU on the work surface, but this occupies space that might be better used. To free up this work space, you might stand it on its side in a floor stand and place it underneath or next to the workstation. You can also purchase a vertical CPU, called a *tower,* that has a much smaller footprint than a standard CPU, occupying less work area. You can stand a tower on the work surface or on the floor, whichever you prefer.

Keyboard — The closer you put the keyboard to your lap, the more comfortable typing will be. If it's placed too high, you must hold your arms up as you work, which can be tiring.

Mount the keyboard at the same height as a typing table, about 24 to 28 inches above the floor. If the work surface is too high to hold the keyboard comfortably, attach a slide-out shelf under the front edge. This shelf should lock in place when it's pulled out so the keyboard won't slide around as you type.

If you spend long stretches of time at your computer, you may want to invest in a pull-out keyboard shelf that can be adjusted up and down. There are even some that swivel. By adjusting the position of the keyboard from time to time, you help to prevent fatigue and ailments caused by repetitive typing movements.

Monitor — There are two schools of thought on where to place the monitor. The most common advice is to place it at eye level. This position relieves strain on the neck, but it also separates the monitor and the keyboard by as much as 60 degrees, as measured from the eye of the operator. This can be tiring as you glance back and forth between components. If you wear bifocals or have trouble focusing, you may be extremely uncomfortable.

Instead, place the monitor as close to the keyboard as possible, the reason being that a little neck strain is better than a lot of eye strain. Some recent computer desk designs include an adjust-

(continued) ▷

DESIGNING A COMPUTER WORKSTATION — CONTINUED

able monitor shelf that drops *below* the level of the keyboard and tilts the monitor upward. As you sit at the workstation, you see the monitor screen just over the top edge of the keyboard — the same position in which you view a piece of paper in a typewriter.

Wherever you place the monitor, the screen should be at least 28 inches from your eyes. Like televisions, monitors generate electromagnetic radiation. Although the medical evidence is not yet conclusive, this radiation may cause cataracts and other vision problems at close range. It may also be harmful to the fetuses of pregnant women. To reduce these dangers, position the monitor as far away from you as practical. If you find it difficult to focus on a screen that's 28 inches away, consider buying eyeglasses.

Printer — The printer is best placed 18 to 24 inches above the floor, lower than the work surface. This lets you reach the printer controls easily *and* lets you read the copy as it rolls out of the machine.

Many workstations provide a separate stand for the printer. If your office space is limited, you can also store it in a large drawer or on a slide-out shelf underneath the work surface. Place the paper beneath the printer, in the bottom of the drawer or on another shelf. To operate the printer, slide it out of the workstation. This arrangement saves space, yet allows you to mount the printer at a comfortable viewing height. You must be careful, however, to turn off the printer before closing the drawer. Otherwise, heat may build up in the drawer and damage the printer's circuits.

Mouse — You must also include a flat area next to your keyboard and at the same level if you will be using a mouse or other pointing device. Because you have to move the mouse to point with it, this space should be four to eight times larger than the mouse itself, depending on how sensitive you've adjusted the pointing device to be. (The more sensitive the mouse, the less space it requires.) If both right- and left-handed people will be using the computer, provide space on *both* sides of the keyboard. If space is precious, consider replacing the mouse with a *trackball*. This performs the same function, but doesn't need to be moved at all.

Wiring and Ventilation — A computer system requires many wires and cables — power cords, printer cables, monitor cables, wires to the keyboard and the mouse. If you have additional components, each of these will probably require a cable and a cord, too. To help organize these wires and make them less obtrusive, consider building hidden channels or a false back into the workstation. Many operators run all the power cords to a power strip so they can turn the entire system off and on with a single switch.

If the workstation encloses any of the computer components, be sure to ventilate the enclosed areas. Provide holes or slots near the top of the cabinet to exhaust the hot air and an equal number of holes or slots near the bottom to let cool air in. If there are a lot of components in a single enclosed space, use a small muffin fan to encourage the air flow.

Other considerations — The placement of other computer components and materials, such as modems, CD-ROM drives, tape backups, speakers, and manuals, isn't as critical. Frequently used items should be within easy reach, either on shelves or in drawers built into the workstation. Arrange things where you won't be tempted to pile other stuff on top of them. It's all too easy to bury small (but important!) items during an absorbing computer session.

Store seldom-used materials in out-of-the-way parts of the workstation. This will help make use of otherwise wasted space. You might, for example, include shelves under the work surface, toward the back, to hold old manuals and full data diskettes.

Perhaps the most important feature you can design into any computer workstation is *flexibility*. As much as possible, make it simple to rearrange or adjust the position of the computer components. There are many ways you can do this. Make the parts of the workstation modular, so they come apart and go back together like building blocks. Make the shelves movable, so you can raise and lower them as needed. This flexibility helps you to keep up with rapidly changing computer technology so you can periodically update your system, adding or replacing components.

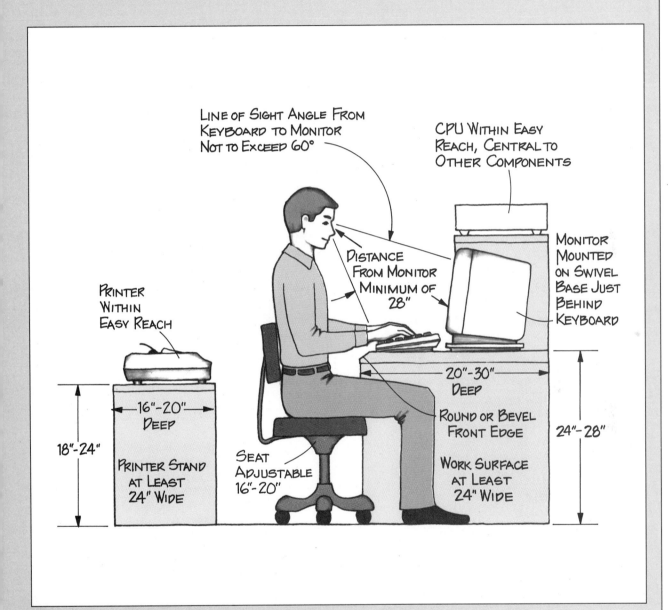

LINE OF SIGHT ANGLE FROM
KEYBOARD TO MONITOR
NOT TO EXCEED 60°

CPU WITHIN EASY
REACH, CENTRAL TO
OTHER COMPONENTS

DISTANCE
FROM MONITOR
MINIMUM OF
28"

MONITOR
MOUNTED
ON SWIVEL
BASE JUST
BEHIND
KEYBOARD

PRINTER
WITHIN
EASY REACH

16"-20"
DEEP

18"-24"

PRINTER STAND
AT LEAST
24" WIDE

SEAT
ADJUSTABLE
16"-20"

20"-30"
DEEP

ROUND OR BEVEL
FRONT EDGE

24"-28"

WORK SURFACE
AT LEAST
24" WIDE

1 **The arrangement of the**
components in a computer system
is just as important, if not more so,
than the components themselves. A
good system, poorly arranged, can
be tedious and uncomfortable to
use. It's the job of the computer desk
or *workstation* to hold all the components in the proper spatial relationship to each other and the operator.

(continued) ▷

DESIGNING A COMPUTER WORKSTATION — CONTINUED

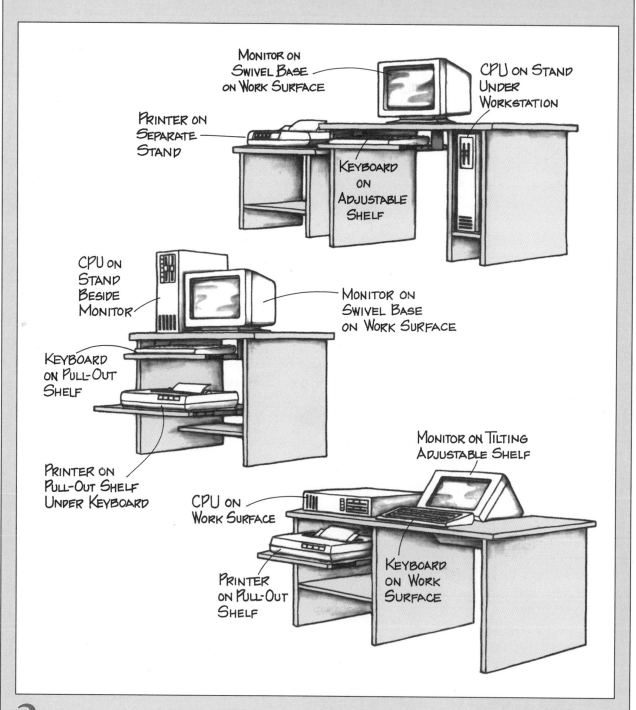

MONITOR ON SWIVEL BASE ON WORK SURFACE

CPU ON STAND UNDER WORKSTATION

PRINTER ON SEPARATE STAND

KEYBOARD ON ADJUSTABLE SHELF

CPU ON STAND BESIDE MONITOR

MONITOR ON SWIVEL BASE ON WORK SURFACE

KEYBOARD ON PULL-OUT SHELF

PRINTER ON PULL-OUT SHELF UNDER KEYBOARD

MONITOR ON TILTING ADJUSTABLE SHELF

CPU ON WORK SURFACE

KEYBOARD ON WORK SURFACE

PRINTER ON PULL-OUT SHELF

2 **Although there are important** rules to follow, no single way to arrange computer components is best. Shown are three possible arrangements that you may find comfortable and productive.

5

MAKING DRAWERS AND PIGEONHOLES

Whereas bookcases are filled with shelves and fitted with doors, desks hold drawers and compartments. Desk drawers come in all shapes and sizes — from small, shallow drawers for stamps, paper clips, and other office supplies to large, deep ones for files and folios. Compartments, on the other hand, are typically small since they are used to organize letters, bills, receipts, and other small items. To make them easier to build and install, these compartments are often grouped together in an arrangement called *pigeonholes.*

MAKING AND INSTALLING DRAWERS

DRAWER CONSTRUCTION

No matter what its size, a desk drawer is an open box and, as such, is built using box joinery. The front, back, and sides are joined at the ends to form a rectangle, and the bottom is attached to this rectangle so as not to stress the corner joints. Some drawers have a sixth part — a false front or drawer *face*. Like doors, drawer fronts and faces can be *inset* inside the desk case; they can *overlay* the case; or they may be *lipped,* so only the lips overlay the case. (*See Figure 5-1.*)

Craftsmen oftentimes use one type of joint to assemble the front corners of the drawer and another for the back. Usually, you don't want to see these joints when the drawer is closed. If this is the case, use simple *rabbets* for the front corners of light-duty drawers. For a slightly stronger assembly, use *lock joints* (also called

tongue-and-dado or double-tongue joints). And for the strongest possible drawers, use *half-blind dovetails* — dovetails that are visible from the side, but not from the front. (*See Figure 5-2.*) If the desk design calls for visible joinery, use something that's visually interesting, such as *through dovetails* or *finger joints.* (*See Figure 5-3.*)

You can use all these joints at the back of the drawer, too, but more often than not, the back corner joinery is much simpler than the front. To join the back to the sides, you might use *dadoes, dado-and-rabbet joints,* or even simple *butt joints.* (*See Figure 5-4.*) The drawer bottom usually floats in *grooves* cut into the inside faces of the other drawer parts. (*See Figures 5-5 and 5-6.*) If the drawer has a false front, it's usually glued or screwed to the drawer front. (*See Figure 5-7.*)

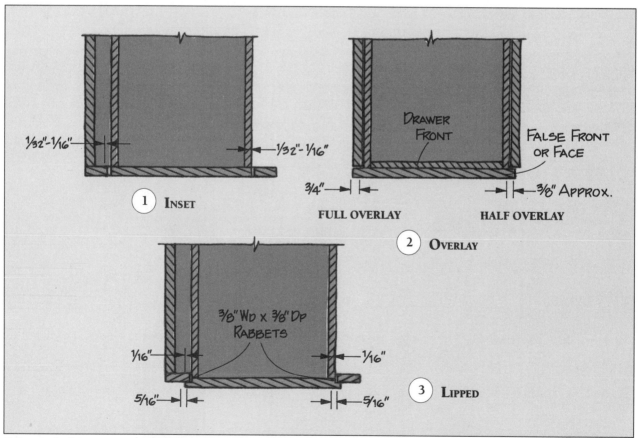

5-1 Desk drawers are open boxes that slide in and out of the desk case. The fronts of these boxes may be *inset* (1) in the case so the drawer front is flush with the face frame or the front edges of the case. The front

can also overlap or *overlay* (2) the case, partially covering the face frame or front edges. (Overlaid drawers often have false fronts or *faces.*) Or the drawer front may be *lipped* (3) — rabbeted all around the perimeter so

only the shoulders of the rabbet fit inside the drawer opening. The lips created by the rabbets overlay the face frame or the front edges.

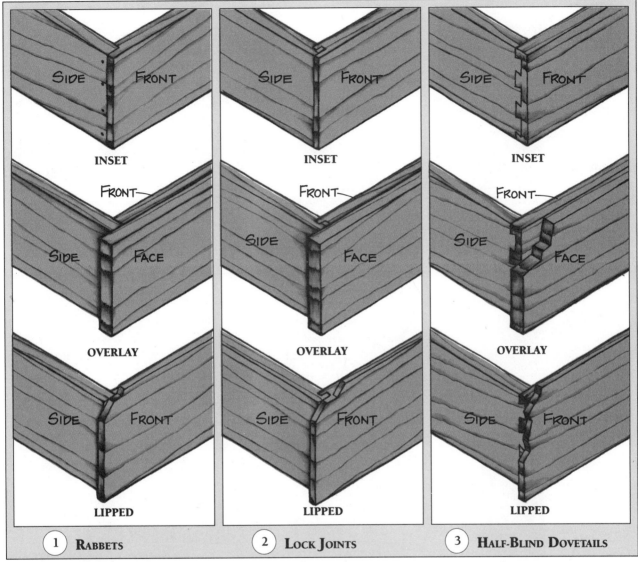

INSET   INSET   INSET

FRONT   FRONT   FRONT

SIDE   FACE   SIDE   FACE   SIDE   FACE

OVERLAY   OVERLAY   OVERLAY

SIDE   FRONT   SIDE   FRONT   SIDE   FRONT

LIPPED   LIPPED   LIPPED

(1) **RABBETS**   (2) **LOCK JOINTS**   (3) **HALF-BLIND DOVETAILS**

5-2 Three joints are commonly used to assemble the front corners of traditional drawers: *rabbets* (1), *lock joints* (2), and *half-blind dovetails* (3). None of these joints are visible from the front. When the drawer is closed, its face appears as a single piece of wood.

5-3 On some recent furniture styles, the joints at the front corners of the drawers are visible and become part of the decoration. For example, the large drawers shown in the photo have *through dovetails* (1), while the smaller ones have *finger joints* (2). Both kinds of joinery appear as light and dark interlocking rectangles near the ends of the drawer fronts when the drawers are closed.

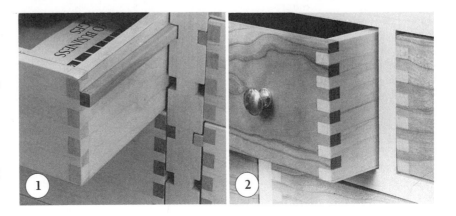

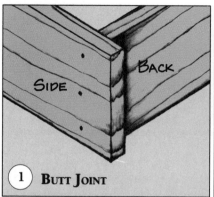

1 BUTT JOINT

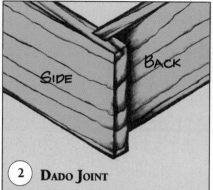

2 DADO JOINT

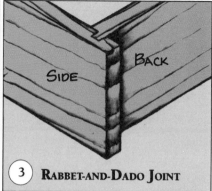

3 RABBET-AND-DADO JOINT

5-4 Because the stress on the back corners of a drawer is much less than on the front, the joinery is often much simpler. For light-duty drawers, you can use simple *butt joints* (1), reinforced with screws or finishing nails, to join the back to the sides. *Dadoes* (2) are slightly stronger, and *rabbet-and-dado joints* (3) are stronger yet. You can also use the same joinery at the back of the drawer as at the front. This will save you setup time, but if the front corner joinery is complex or time-consuming to make, it may not save you time overall.

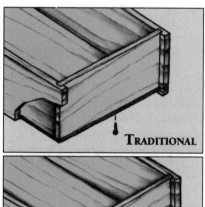

TRADITIONAL

MODERN

5-5 A desk drawer bottom normally floats in grooves so it can expand and contract without stress-ing the corner joints. A traditional drawer is designed so you can slide the bottom into grooves in the sides and front, then nail or screw the bot-tom to the back. This is done after you've assembled the front, back, and sides. On a modern drawer, the bottom rests in grooves in the front, sides, *and* back. All the parts must be assembled at the same time. **Note:** Traditional drawers usually have solid wood bottoms, and modern drawers have plywood bottoms.

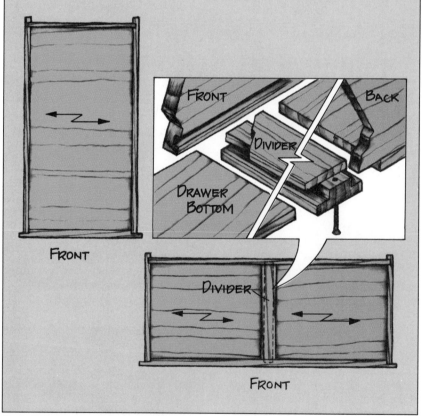

5-6 When you make a traditional drawer with a solid wood bottom, the grain direction should run from side to side so the drawer bottom will expand toward the back. If the drawer is extremely wide, break up the bottom into two or more sections and join the sections with *dividers,* as shown. This will keep the drawer bottom from sagging. **Note:** Some-times the undersides of drawer dividers are grooved to follow guides, as shown in *FIGURE 5-10*.

5-7 If a drawer has a false front or false face, wait until *after* you've hung the drawer in the desk to attach it. Then temporarily attach the face to the drawer front with double-faced carpet tape. When you're satisfied with the position of the face, drill two pilot holes from the *inside* of the drawer, through the front, and into the face — these holes will help you to position the face when you glue it in place. Remove the face, discard the tape, and apply glue to the drawer front. Replace the face, lining up the holes and driving screws through them. Use these screws to hold the face in position until the glue dries.

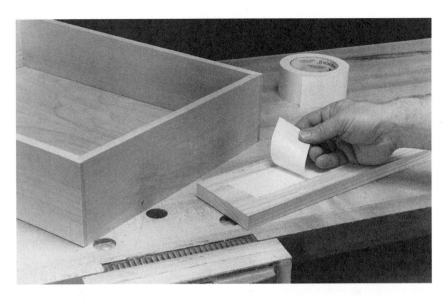

FOR YOUR INFORMATION

Most traditional and modern drawer designs call for the drawer sides to extend $1/4$ to $1/2$ inch past the drawer back. This makes the drawer simpler to build and slightly stronger than if the ends of the side are flush with the back. For inset drawers, the back ends of the sides often serve as stops to keep the drawer from being pushed too far into the desk case. The sides make more stable stops than the back. Should the back cup or warp, the drawer may protrude from the case slightly. Should the sides cup, the position of the drawer won't be affected.

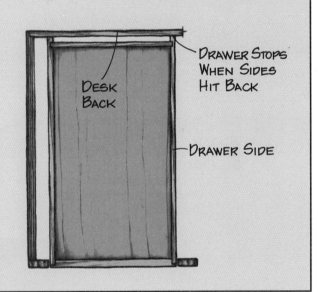

DESK BACK

DRAWER STOPS WHEN SIDES HIT BACK

DRAWER SIDE

INSTALLING DRAWERS

There are many ways that you might hang drawers in a desk, but five methods are used most often (*SEE FIGURE 5-8):*

■ *Shelves* — The drawers rest on solid boards. As they slide in and out of the case, they are guided by rails, dividers, or the sides of the case. (*SEE FIGURE 5-9.*)

■ *Web frames* — Web frames work like shelves — that is, they provide a horizontal surface for the drawers to rest on. However, they aren't solid boards like shelves. To conserve materials and improve stability, they are made up of rails, stiles, and panels. (*SEE FIGURE 5-10.*)

■ *Brackets* — The drawers are cradled in L-shaped brackets that not only support the drawers, but guide them as they slide in and out of the case. (*SEE FIGURE 5-11.*)

■ *Side-mounted guides* — The sides of the drawer are grooved to fit over wooden strips or guides, which are mounted to the sides of the case. Like brackets, these strips support and direct the drawers. (*SEE FIGURE 5-12.*)

■ *Extension slides* — This hardware mounts to the drawer sides and desk case to support and guide the drawer. *Full-extension slides* are especially useful for installing file drawers because they allow you to pull a drawer all the way out of a desk. This, in turn, lets you reach the files in the back of the drawer. (SEE FIGURES 5-13 THROUGH 5-15.)

If you install a drawer on a shelf, web frame, or brackets, you may also have to install *kickers* above the drawer. These pieces keep the drawer from tipping forward when you slide it out of the desk case. (SEE FIGURE 5-16.) The wooden parts above some drawers serve as kickers. In a typical pedestal desk, for example, each pair of brackets supports a drawer *and* keeps the drawer below from tipping. However, the top drawer in each pedestal has no brackets above it and requires kickers.

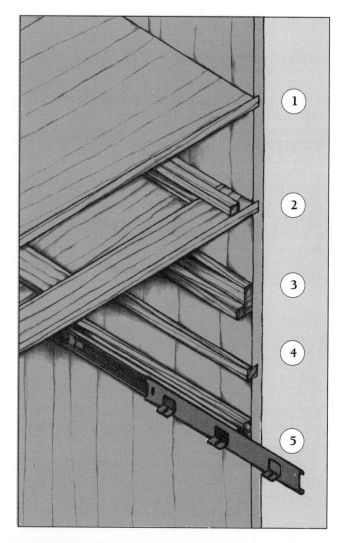

5-8 There are five common ways to hang desk drawers. Rest them on a *shelf* (1) or a *web frame* (2); suspend them from L-shaped *brackets* (3) or *side-mounted guides* (4); or attach them with *extension slides* (5).

5-9 Small drawers, such as those in the top portion of this table desk, are often supported on simple *shelves*. As you slide the drawers in and out of the desk, they are guided by the case sides or dividers. In some desks, tiny drawers fill the compartments in pigeonholes and are supported and guided by the pigeonhole shelves and dividers. However, this is not a practical method for installing large drawers. It would require too much material, which would add to the expense and weight of the desk.

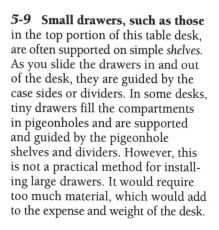

5-10 Large desk drawers often rest on *web frames*. The rails and stiles of these frames are joined by tongue-and-groove joinery, as shown. The voids in the frames are sometimes filled with dust panels — sheets of thin material that prevent dust and dirt from settling on the items stored beneath the drawer. The drawers are guided by strips of wood, or guides, attached to the top surface of the frame. You can use two guides per drawer, one on either side, or a single center guide under each drawer. If you use a center guide, build each drawer with a divider in the bottom and cut a groove in the divider to fit the guide.

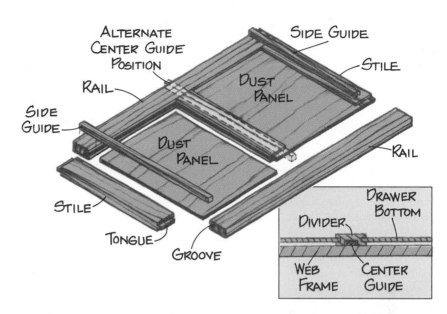

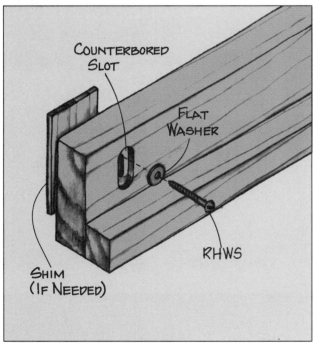

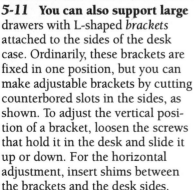

5-11 You can also support large drawers with L-shaped *brackets* attached to the sides of the desk case. Ordinarily, these brackets are fixed in one position, but you can make adjustable brackets by cutting counterbored slots in the sides, as shown. To adjust the vertical position of a bracket, loosen the screws that hold it in the desk and slide it up or down. For the horizontal adjustment, insert shims between the brackets and the desk sides.

5-12 When drawer space is at a premium and you must stack two or more drawers vertically in a desk, use *side-mounted guides* to hang them. These guides are glued in dadoes in the desk sides, and the drawer sides are grooved to fit over the guides. The drawers are supported from the sides, so you don't have to put shelves, frames, or brackets between the drawers. You can hang deeper drawers or more of them in the same vertical space.

5-13 **To install *extension slides*,** build the drawer narrower than you would otherwise. The front of the drawer should be the same width as the drawer opening, but the overall width at the sides must be less to accommodate the hardware. (Most slides are ½ inch wide. Since you need two slides for each drawer, the drawer must be 1 inch narrower than the drawer opening.) The surfaces inside the desk to which you will attach the slides must be flush with the sides of the drawer opening. If not, install spacers or mounting plates that are flush.

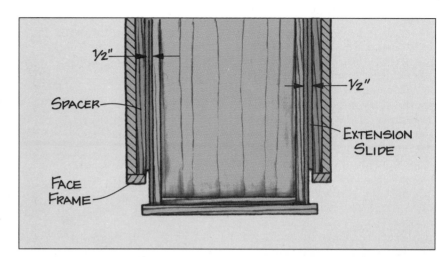

5-14 **Disassemble each slide into** two pieces — the drawer bracket and the extension mechanism. Carefully measure and mark the positions of both parts on the drawer sides and the inside of the desk case. Remember, the slides must be perfectly parallel to operate smoothly. Install the hardware, screwing the brackets to the drawer and the extension mechanisms inside the desk. **Note:** There are two types of mounting holes in most extension slides — round and slotted. Mount the hardware using the *slotted holes only* until you are sure the slides are positioned properly. Also, drive the screws through the center of the slots — this will let you adjust the guide in either direction.

5-15 **Reassemble the brackets** and the extension mechanisms, then slide the drawer in and out of the case several times to check that the slides are positioned correctly. If the drawer rubs on the desk case, the slides are too high or too low. If it binds, the slides aren't parallel. Loosen the screws that hold the brackets or extension mechanisms in place, shift the hardware slightly, and check again. When the slides are positioned properly, install screws in the *round* mounting holes.

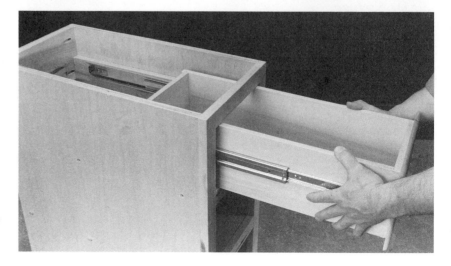

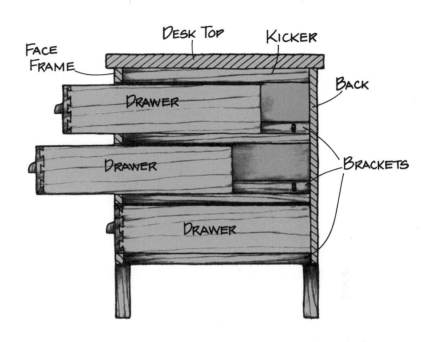

5-16 However you install desk drawers, you must make sure they don't tip forward when you slide them out of the case. Side-mounted guides and extension slides take care of this problem for you, but if you use shelves, web frames, or brackets, you may have to install strips of wood called *kickers* to control tipping. In desks where the drawers are stacked vertically, the frame or the bracket *above* a drawer may keep it from tipping. However, the top drawer may still require kickers.

TRY THIS TRICK

When you install drawers in a desk, fasten a turn button to the back of each drawer. Flip the turn button up after sliding the drawer in place so it catches on the face frame when you pull the drawer forward. This will prevent you from accidentally pulling the drawer out of the desk. If you have to remove the drawer, flip the turn button down. **Note:** If you make the turn button long enough, it will also serve as a kicker, keeping the drawer from tipping forward.

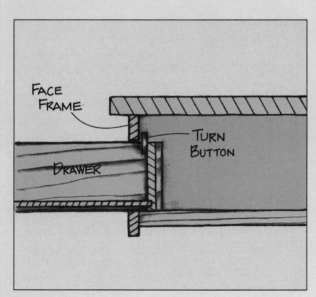

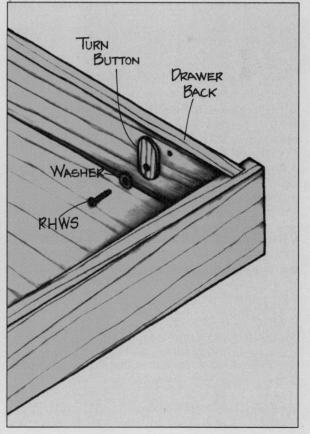

MAKING PIGEONHOLES

The prevailing method for building pigeonholes has changed over the years. Up until the mid-nineteenth century, shelves and dividers were typically double-mitered on the ends to make them pointed, and the points rested in V-shaped grooves. Often, the front edges were rounded. *(SEE FIGURE 5-17.)* After the Civil War, craftsmen began building pigeonholes like tiny shelving units, in which the shelves and dividers rest in ordinary dadoes and rabbets. *(SEE FIGURE 5-18.)*

Although pigeonholes can be joined to the desk case like fixed shelves, they are sometimes built as separate units, then installed inside the case with fasteners or molding. Craftsmen often use this construction method when making rolltop desks. The pigeonholes are set inside the tamboured case, but the two assemblies are built separately. If either unit requires repair, the pigeonholes can be easily removed from the case. *(SEE FIGURE 5-19.)*

5-17 Pigeonholes in Queen Anne-, Federal-, and other classic-style desks were often assembled with *toe joints.* The ends of the shelves and dividers were double-mitered to create pointed tenons, or *toes,* which rested in matching V-shaped grooves and notches. Old-time craftsmen cut these tenons and grooves with special matched molding planes. You can reproduce the same joints with a table-mounted router and a V-groove bit. Cut the toes on the ends of the pigeonhole parts with two passes over the bit, then rout the grooves in a single pass.

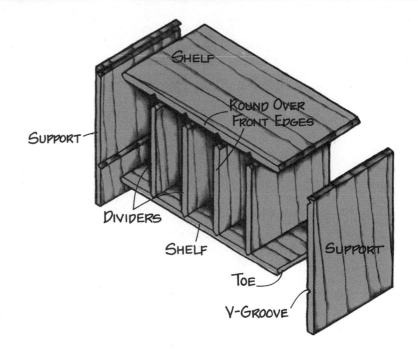

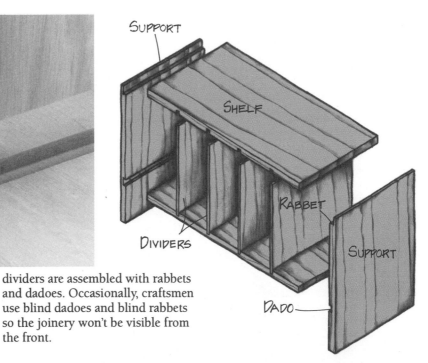

5-18 As the woodworking trades have become more mechanized, desk joinery has changed so it can be easily made with power tools. Nowadays, pigeonholes are built like miniature shelving units — the shelves and dividers are assembled with rabbets and dadoes. Occasionally, craftsmen use blind dadoes and blind rabbets so the joinery won't be visible from the front.

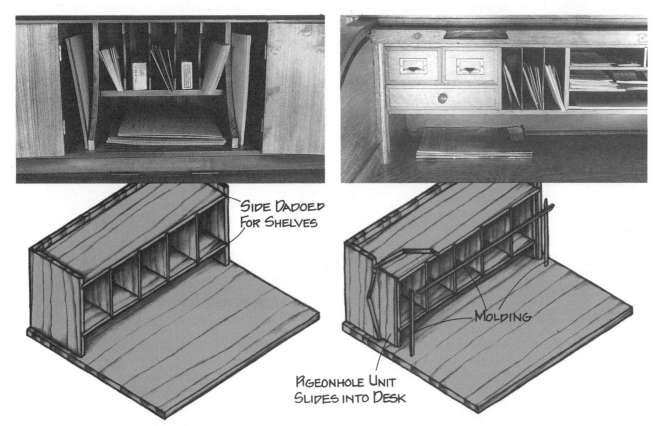

5-19 There are two ways that you might install pigeonholes in a desk. On the table desk *(above left)*, the pigeonholes are built into the case and are an integrated part of the structure. They cannot be removed since they are joined permanently. On the rolltop desk *(above right)*, the pigeonholes are built as a separate unit. They are inserted in the case and held in place with molding.

SECRET COMPARTMENTS

In addition to pigeonholes and other easily accessible compartments, you might also consider building one or two *secret* compartments in your desk. There are many places to conceal a compartment, provided you have unused space in the desk. The trick is to make it look as if this space were utilized for more obvious and mundane purposes. Here are four possible ways to do this:

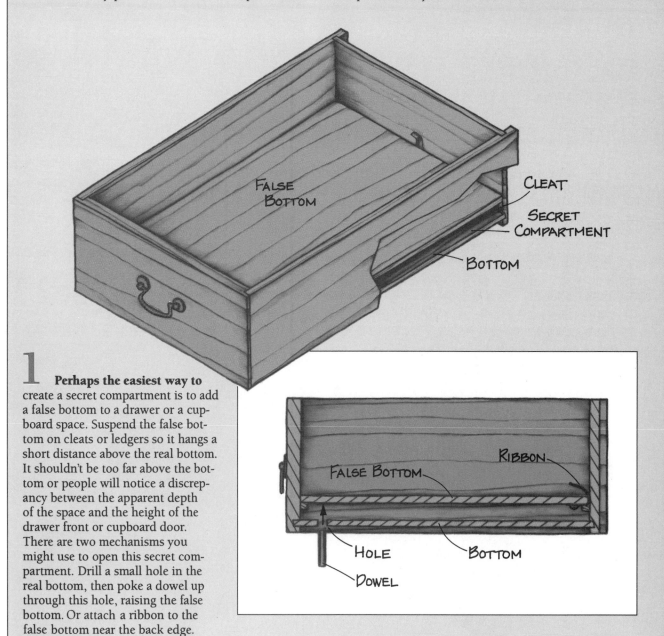

1 **Perhaps the easiest way to** create a secret compartment is to add a false bottom to a drawer or a cupboard space. Suspend the false bottom on cleats or ledgers so it hangs a short distance above the real bottom. It shouldn't be too far above the bottom or people will notice a discrepancy between the apparent depth of the space and the height of the drawer front or cupboard door. There are two mechanisms you might use to open this secret compartment. Drill a small hole in the real bottom, then poke a dowel up through this hole, raising the false bottom. Or attach a ribbon to the false bottom near the back edge. When you lay the false bottom in place, make sure a small portion of the ribbon remains visible — just enough to grab on to.

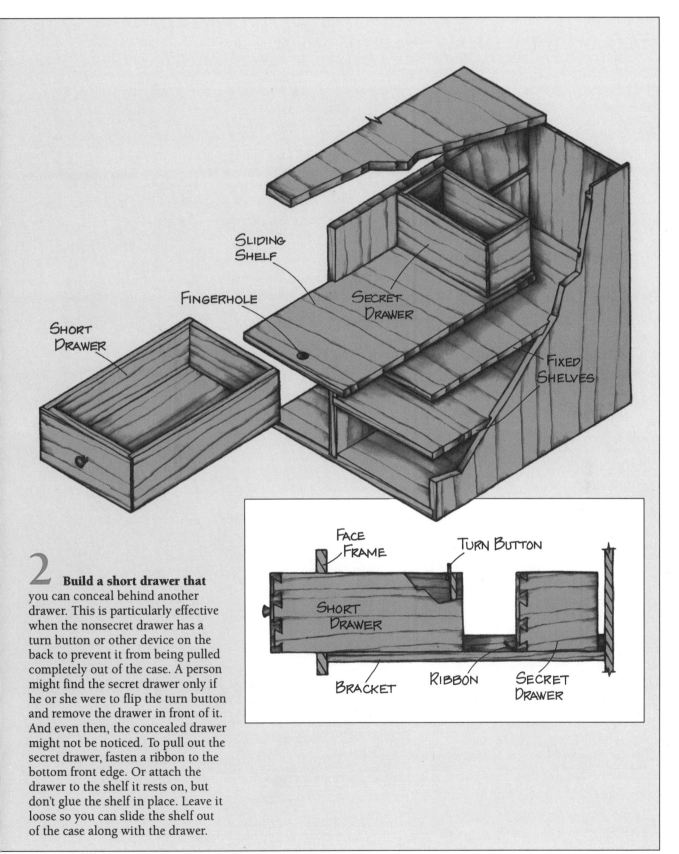

SLIDING SHELF

FINGERHOLE

SHORT DRAWER

SECRET DRAWER

FIXED SHELVES

FACE FRAME

TURN BUTTON

SHORT DRAWER

BRACKET

RIBBON

SECRET DRAWER

2 **Build a short drawer that** you can conceal behind another drawer. This is particularly effective when the nonsecret drawer has a turn button or other device on the back to prevent it from being pulled completely out of the case. A person might find the secret drawer only if he or she were to flip the turn button and remove the drawer in front of it. And even then, the concealed drawer might not be noticed. To pull out the secret drawer, fasten a ribbon to the bottom front edge. Or attach the drawer to the shelf it rests on, but don't glue the shelf in place. Leave it loose so you can slide the shelf out of the case along with the drawer.

(continued) ▷

SECRET COMPARTMENTS — CONTINUED

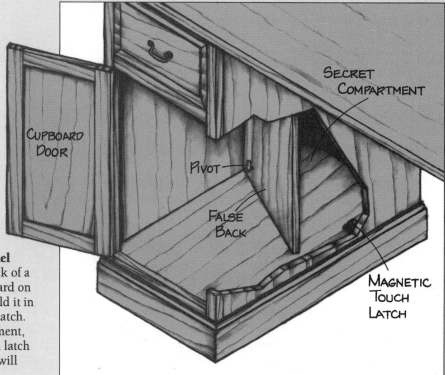

3 **Install a movable panel** behind a drawer or in the back of a compartment. Mount this board on pivots or knife hinges and hold it in place with a magnetic touch latch. To access the secret compartment, push on the panel. The touch latch will pop open and the board will swing out of the way.

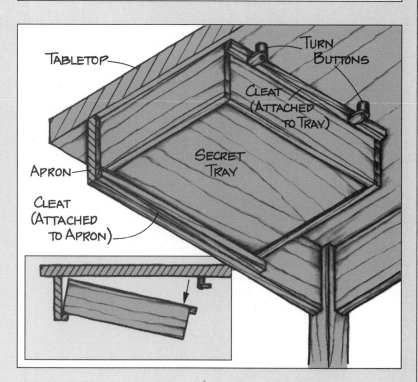

4 **You don't have to build a** massive desk with drawers and pigeonholes to make secret compartments. You can create secret spaces in something as simple as a writing table by building a box or a tray that rests just below the work surface, where it will be concealed by the aprons. Attach cleats to the aprons to hold one side of the tray, and screw turn buttons to the underside of the work surface to hold the other side. To remove the tray, rotate the turn buttons and let it drop down.

MAKING TAMBOURS

Oftentimes pigeonholes in desks are enclosed with a *tamboured* door — narrow strips of wood strung together with cloth or other materials. These strips make a flexible panel that slides in grooves. The rolltop on a rolltop desk is the best-known example of a tamboured door — as you open the rolltop, the tambours slide in a curved groove, disappearing out of sight into the top of the desk.

A tamboured door works well with pigeonholes for several reasons. Unlike a hinged door, it doesn't

swing out across the desk surface; consequently, you don't have to move things on your desk to open it. And unlike a sliding door, which always leaves a portion of the pigeonholes covered, tamboured doors provide unobstructed access when open. Finally, if you build an *inset* pigeonhole unit (as shown on page 77) and leave a cavity between the back of the pigeonholes and the desk back, you can use this space to hold the door when you open it. The tambours will seem to vanish behind the pigeonholes.

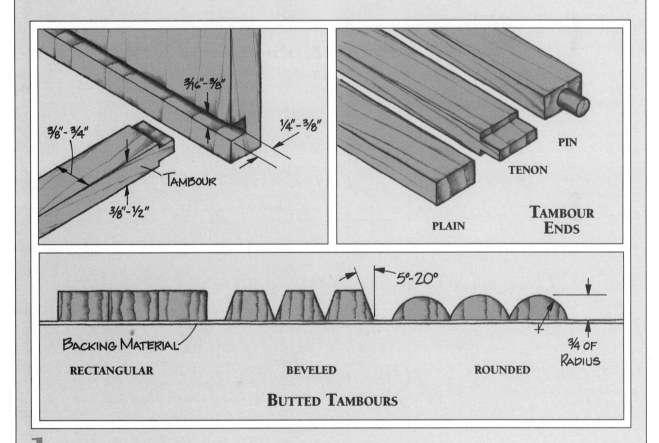

1 **Tambours are slender strips** of wood, generally 3/8 to 1/2 inch thick and 3/8 to 3/4 inch wide. The ends of the tambours ride in grooves that are 3/16 to 3/8 inch wide and 1/4 to 3/8 inch deep. Tambours are butted together and glued to the backing material with the edges touching.

You can make tambours in several shapes — rectangular, beveled, and rounded are the most common. In addition, you can cut tenons or install wooden pins on the ends of the tambours to ride in the grooves, if you choose.

(continued) ▷

MAKING TAMBOURS — CONTINUED

2 **The grooves in which the** tambours travel are always curved. When designing a tamboured door and the grooves it rides in, make sure that the tambours can follow the curves. Rectangular tambours can only travel around outside curves; rounded tambours can follow outside curves, but only *gentle* inside curves; and, depending on the angle of the bevel, beveled tambours can follow inside and outside curves with equal ease. In addition, the radius of the curves must not be too small. The gentler the curve, the easier it will be for the tambours to follow. If the curve is too sharp, the corners of the tambours or the tenons may bind. **Note:** To test your design, make a small tamboured door just 6 inches square, rout a trial groove in a scrap of plywood, and see if you can push the tambours along the groove easily.

3 **The lengths of both the** tamboured door and the grooves in which it rides are critical. The door must be long enough to cover the opening, and the grooves must be long enough for the door to open completely. To calculate these lengths, lay out the full-size groove design on a scrap of plywood. Tack brads or finishing nails along the center of the groove every 1 inch. Weave a measuring tape along the nails to find the approximate length of the groove. From this, calculate the length of the door — normally, it should be a little longer than half the length of the groove. You may wish to cut a string to represent the door and weave it along the nails in both the open and closed position. If necessary, adjust the length of the groove or the door until you find a combination that works.

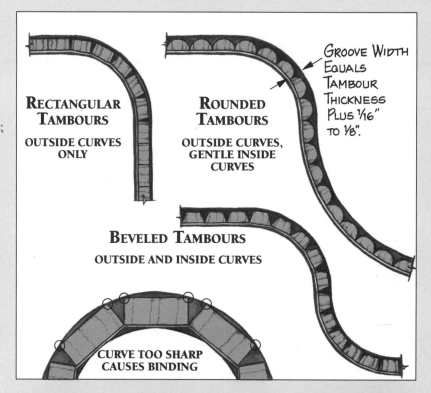

RECTANGULAR
TAMBOURS

OUTSIDE CURVES
ONLY

ROUNDED
TAMBOURS

OUTSIDE CURVES,
GENTLE INSIDE
CURVES

GROOVE WIDTH
EQUALS
TAMBOUR
THICKNESS
PLUS 1/16"
TO 1/8".

BEVELED TAMBOURS

OUTSIDE AND INSIDE CURVES

CURVE TOO SHARP
CAUSES BINDING

4 **Select the clearest, straightest** lumber you can find to make the tambours. Plan on making about one-third more tambours than you actually need, because many of the tambours you cut won't be straight enough to use. Even clear, straight lumber hides *reaction wood* — wood with internal stresses that bows or twists after you cut it. Plane the wood to thickness, joint an edge, and cut it about an inch longer than you need. Rip the tambours, jointing the cut edge between each rip. Stack the tambours and let them dry for several days to equalize the moisture content. (Depending on the season, tambours cut from the center of a board may be slightly wetter or drier than those cut from the edge.) After drying the tambours, inspect them. A gentle curve is acceptable, but discard those pieces that are badly bowed and require a lot of pressure to straighten.

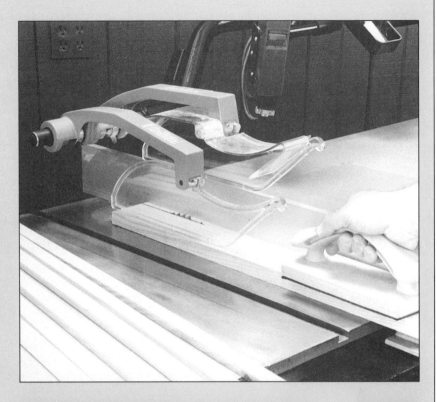

5 **If your design requires it,** shape the tambour stock with a table-mounted router. It's normally not good shop practice to shape slender stock; however, you have to in this case because the tambours must be dried and inspected before they can be used. To shape the tambours safely, make a simple jig to cradle them as you feed them past the router bit — a single block of wood with a rabbet or a groove cut in it the same size as the tambours. Clamp the jig to the router table fence with the cutout facing the bit. Feed the tambours into one end of the jig and out the other.

(continued) ▷

MAKING TAMBOURS — CONTINUED

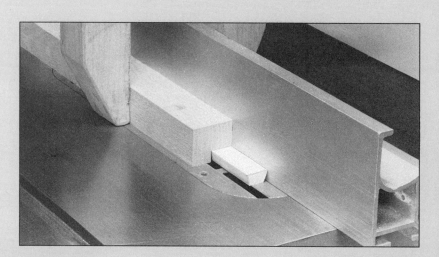

6 **If required, cut bevels or** rabbets in the tambours with a table saw or radial arm saw. Again, use a grooved or rabbeted board to help guide the tambours past the saw blade. Clamp this fixture to the table saw fence or radial arm saw backstop.

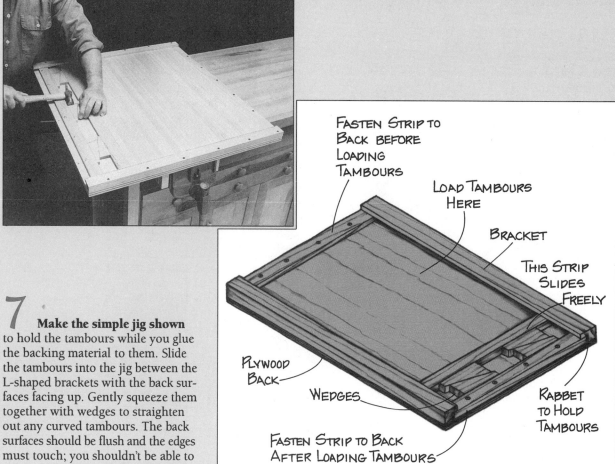

7 **Make the simple jig shown** to hold the tambours while you glue the backing material to them. Slide the tambours into the jig between the L-shaped brackets with the back surfaces facing up. Gently squeeze them together with wedges to straighten out any curved tambours. The back surfaces should be flush and the edges must touch; you shouldn't be able to see any gaps between the tambours.

FASTEN STRIP TO BACK BEFORE LOADING TAMBOURS

LOAD TAMBOURS HERE

BRACKET

THIS STRIP SLIDES FREELY

PLYWOOD BACK

WEDGES

FASTEN STRIP TO BACK AFTER LOADING TAMBOURS

RABBET TO HOLD TAMBOURS

8   **You can use muslin, silk,** linen, or leather as a backing material for the tambours. (Ten-ounce unsized muslin, available at most fabric and art supply stores, is the most common choice.) Cut the material about 3 inches longer than the length of the door (as measured *across* the tambours) and 2 inches shorter than the tambours themselves (as measured *along* the tambours). After protecting your workbench with a sheet of plastic, lay out the backing material and mask off 3 inches near the end where you will later attach the handle. Apply white or yellow glue to the backing. Don't use too much — the backing materials should be saturated but not dripping with glue. With a helper, peel up the backing, turn it over (glue side down), and position it on the

tambours, letting the masked portion overhang the last tambour. Carefully spread the backing so there are no wrinkles, trim the edges straight with a razor or sharp knife, and let

the glue dry. **Note:** If you apply glue directly to the tambours and press the backing in place, you may force adhesive between the tambours and glue the edges together.

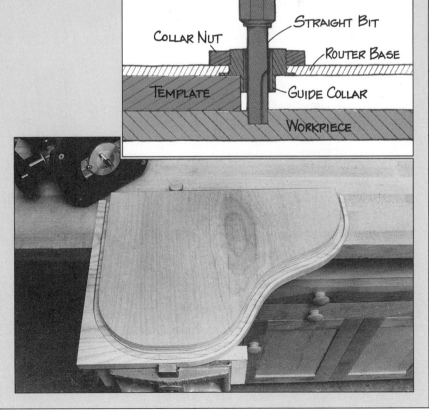

9   **Cut a template to guide the** router as you cut the grooves for the tambours. This template should be the same profile as the grooves, but slightly smaller to allow for the difference in diameters between the guide collar and the router bit. Attach the guide collar to the router base and mount the bit, making sure the bit is centered in the collar. Affix the template to a desk side with double-faced carpet tape, and rout the groove in several passes, cutting just $^1/_{16}$ to $^1/_8$ inch deeper with each pass. Remove the template, turn it over, and repeat for the second desk side.

(continued) ▷

MAKING TAMBOURS — CONTINUED

10 **Assemble the desk case** and carefully measure the space between the sides *at several points* along the grooves — it should not vary more than $1/8$ inch. Remove the tambour assembly from the gluing jig and affix the backing to a scrap of plywood or fiberboard with double-faced carpet tape. Calculate the length of the tambours — take the *shortest* distance between the sides, add *twice* the depth of the grooves, and subtract $1/16$ inch. For example, if the shortest distance between the sides is 36 inches, and the depth of the grooves is $3/8$ inch, the tambours should be $36^{11}/16$ inches long:

$$36 + (2 \times {}^3/_8) - {}^1/_{16} = 36^{11}/_{16}.$$

With the assembly stuck to the scrap, cut the tambours to length. If required, also cut tenons or drill holes for pins. Then remove the tambours from the scrap and discard the tape.

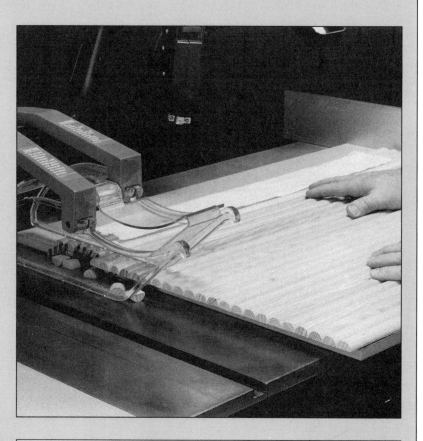

11 **To finish the tamboured** door, you must install a *handle*. Make this from a long strip of wood that is the same length as the tambours, but slightly wider and thicker. If the tambours have plain ends, cut tenons in the ends of the handle to fit it to the grooves. If the tambours have tenons or pins, cut matching tenons or install the same size pins in the handle. Shape the handle to provide a purchase for your fingers. Remove the masking tape from the canvas flap that overhangs the last tambour and attach the handle to it. Slide the completed tamboured door into its grooves in the desk case. When you finish the desk, apply finish sparingly inside the grooves. Wax the tambour ends and the grooves so the door will slide easily.

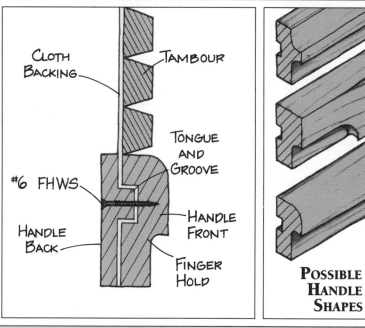

CLOTH BACKING

TAMBOUR

TONGUE AND GROOVE

#6 FHWS

HANDLE FRONT

HANDLE BACK

FINGER HOLD

POSSIBLE HANDLE SHAPES

PROJECTS

6

COUNTRY LETTER DESK

The letter desk is a popular country design — a small table desk made especially for correspondence and paying bills. The table that supports the desk is similar to many nineteenth-century worktables. The aprons form the sides of a large bin, and the work surface is split into two parts and hinged to provide access to materials stored in the bin.

The writing box, which rests on the table, provides a different kind of storage. In the center of the box there are pigeonholes for letters, bills, and files. At either end there are small drawers for paper clips, stamps, and other office supplies.

Note: As shown, this desk is designed for writing and book-keeping. However, you can adapt it to hold a computer simply by altering the dimensions. See "Variations" at the end of this chapter.

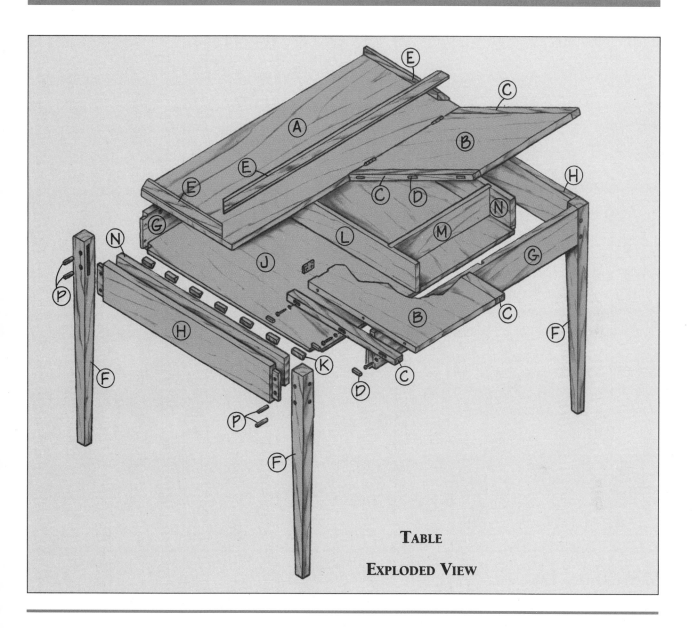

TABLE

EXPLODED VIEW

MATERIALS LIST (FINISHED DIMENSIONS)

Parts

Table

A. Tabletop $3/4'' \times 14\frac{1}{2}'' \times 38''$
B. Lids (2) $3/4'' \times 11\frac{1}{2}'' \times 16\frac{1}{2}''$
C. Breadboard
    ends (4) $3/4'' \times 1\frac{1}{4}'' \times 11\frac{1}{2}''$
D. Plugs (12) $3/8'' \times 1\frac{1}{4}'' \times \frac{1}{2}''$
E. Molding (total) $1'' \times 1'' \times 66''$
F. Legs (4) $1\frac{3}{4}'' \times 1\frac{3}{4}'' \times 28\frac{1}{4}''$
G. Front/back
    aprons (2) $3/4'' \times 5'' \times 34''$
H. Side aprons (2) $3/4'' \times 5'' \times 23''$

J. Table
    bottom* $1/2'' \times 23\frac{1}{2}'' \times 34\frac{1}{2}''$
K. Glue
    blocks (34) $3/4'' \times 3/4'' \times 2\frac{1}{2}''$
L. Long
    divider $3/4'' \times 3\frac{3}{4}'' \times 24\frac{1}{4}''$
M. Short
    divider $3/4'' \times 3\frac{3}{4}'' \times 17\frac{1}{4}''$
N. Spacers (2) $3/4'' \times 3\frac{3}{4}'' \times 21\frac{1}{2}''$
P. Pegs (16) $3/16'' \times 3/16'' \times 1''$

Hardware

Table

#12 x 1½" Roundhead wood
  screws (12)

3/16" Flat washers (12)

#10 x 1¼" Flathead wood screws
  (8)

4d Finishing nails (8–10)

1½" x 2" Butt hinges and mounting screws (2 pairs)

*Make this part from plywood.

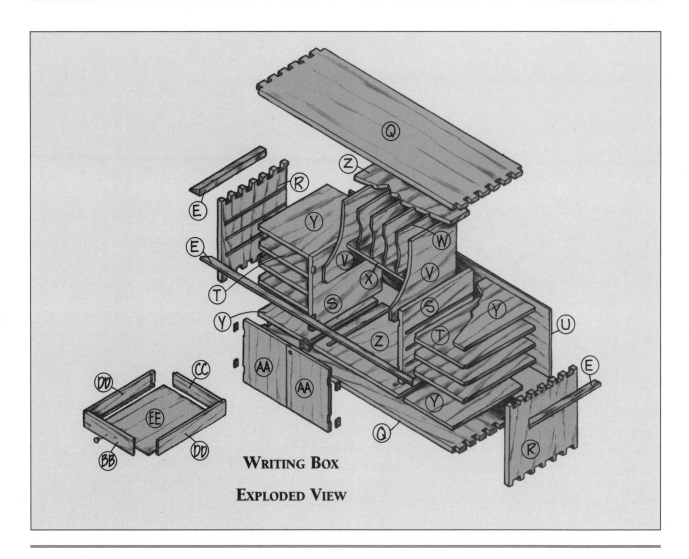

WRITING BOX

EXPLODED VIEW

MATERIALS LIST (FINISHED DIMENSIONS)

Parts

Writing Box

E. Molding (total)   1″ x 1″ x 66″
Q. Box top/
    bottom (2)   ¾″ x 12¾″ x 36″
R. Box sides (2)   ¾″ x 12¾″ x 12″
S. Box dividers
    (2)   ¾″ x 12½″ x 10½″
T. Shelves (6)   ½″ x 12½″ x 9¼″
U. Back*   ¼″ x 11″ x 35″
V. Tall pigeonhole
    dividers (2)   ½″ x 12″ x 10″
W. Short pigeonhole
    dividers (4)   ¼″ x 7¼″ x 6″
X. Pigeonhole
    shelf   ½″ x 7¼″ x 11½″

Y. Drawer
    spacers (4)   ½″ x 12½″ x 8¾″
Z. Pigeonhole
    spacers (2)   ½″ x 12½″ x 15½″
AA. Pigeonhole
    doors (2)   ½″ x 7¹⁵/₁₆″ x 9⁷/₁₆″
BB. Drawer
    fronts (8)   ³/₈″ x 1¹⁵/₁₆″ x 8¹¹/₁₆″
CC. Drawer
    backs (8)   ¼″ x 1¹¹/₁₆″ x 8⁷/₁₆″
DD. Drawer
    sides (16)   ¼″ x 1¹⁵/₁₆″ x 12³/₈″
EE. Drawer bottoms*
    (8)   ⅛″ x 8⁷/₁₆″ x 11⁷/₈″

Hardware

Writing Box

4d Finishing nails (8–10)
1″ Wire brads (16–20)
¾″ Wire nails (8)
1″ x 1½″ Butt hinges and mount-
    ing screws (2 pairs)
¾″ dia. Pulls (8)
Small door lock

Make these parts from plywood.

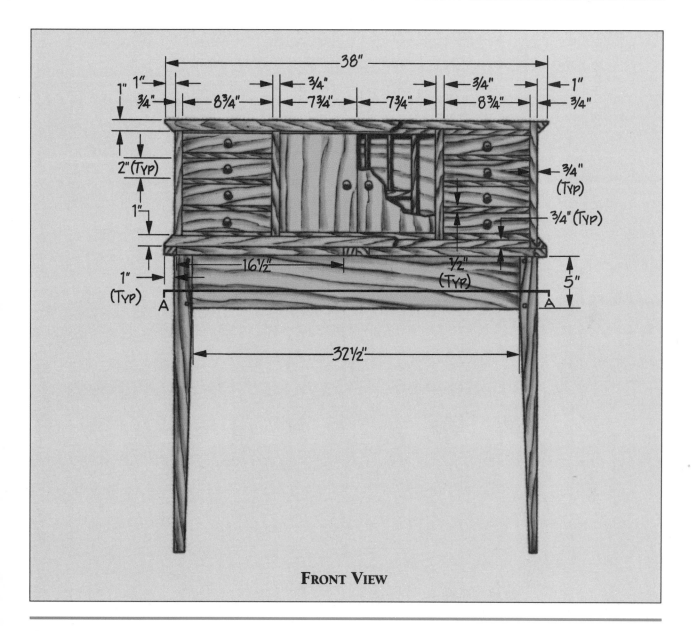

FRONT VIEW

PLAN OF PROCEDURE

1 **Select the stock.** To make the letter desk, you need about 45 board feet of 4/4 (four-quarters) stock, 6 board feet of 8/4 (eight-quarters) stock, one-quarter sheet (2 feet by 4 feet) of ½-inch plywood, one-quarter sheet of ¼-inch plywood, and one-quarter sheet of ⅛-inch plywood. You can use almost any type of wood and cabinet-grade plywood, but walnut, cherry, maple, poplar, and white pine are the traditional choices for country-style projects. The desk shown is made mostly from poplar and birch-veneer plywood. The pegs that hold the aprons to the legs are made from maple.

MAKING THE TABLE

2 **Cut the table parts to size.** Plane the 8/4 stock to 1¾ inches thick and cut the legs from it. From the remaining 1¾-inch-thick lumber, rip 1-inch-square strips to make the molding. Don't cut the molding to length yet.

Plane the 4/4 stock to ¾ inch thick and cut the remaining solid wood parts for the table to the measurements given in the Materials List, except for the glue blocks. Set stock aside for these, but don't make them yet. Cut the table bottom from ½-inch plywood, and cut the pegs from an extremely hard wood such as rock maple or hickory.

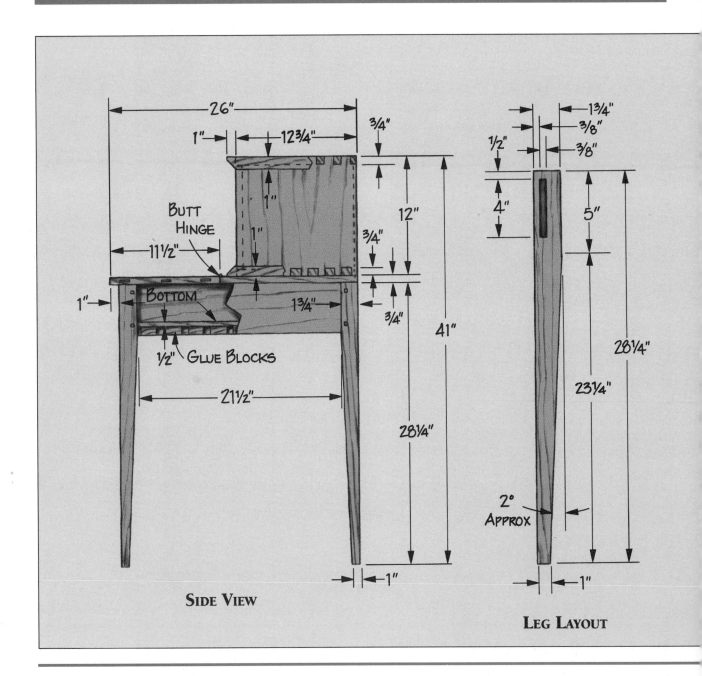

SIDE VIEW

LEG LAYOUT

3 **Cut the mortises and tenons in the legs and aprons.** Using a router, a mortiser, or a drill press, cut 3/8-inch-wide, 4-inch-long, 3/4-inch-deep mortises in the inside surfaces of the legs, as shown in the *Leg Layout* and *Leg-to-Apron Joinery Detail*. Cut tenons in the ends of the aprons with a router or dado cutter. Note that when the mortises and tenons are assembled, the outside faces of the legs and aprons are flush with one another.

4 **Cut the mortises in the breadboard ends.** While you're set up to make mortises, cut 3/8-inch-wide, 3/4-inch-deep, 1 1/4-inch-long mortises in the breadboard ends, as shown in the *Breadboard End Layout/Side View* and *Lid Joinery Detail*. In the center of each mortise, make a 3/16-inch-wide, 1/2-inch-long slot through the board. Later, you'll use these slots and mortises to attach the breadboard ends to the lids.

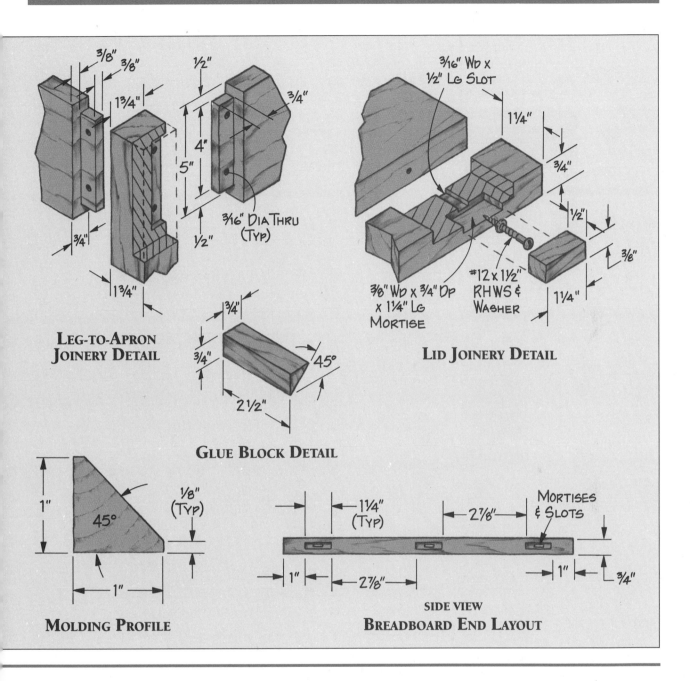

LEG-TO-APRON JOINERY DETAIL

3/8" 3/8"
1 3/4"
4"
5"
1/2"
3/4"
1 3/4"
1/2"
3/4"
3/16" Dia Thru (Typ)

LID JOINERY DETAIL

3/16" Wd x 1/2" Lg Slot
1 1/4"
3/4"
1/2"
3/8"
1 1/4"
3/8" Wd x 3/4" Dp x 1 1/4" Lg Mortise
#12 x 1 1/2" RHWS & Washer

GLUE BLOCK DETAIL

3/4"
3/4"
45°
2 1/2"

MOLDING PROFILE

1"
45°
1/8" (Typ)
1"

SIDE VIEW BREADBOARD END LAYOUT

1 1/4" (Typ)
2 7/8"
Mortises & Slots
1"
2 7/8"
1"
3/4"

5 **Cut dadoes in the aprons, spacer, and long divider.** The long divider is held in dadoes in the front and back aprons, while the short divider is held in dadoes in the long divider and a spacer, as shown in *Section A*. Cut these 3/4-inch-wide, 3/8-inch-deep dadoes with a router or dado cutter.

6 **Taper the legs.** The legs taper from 1 3/4 inches square at the top to 1 inch square at the bottom, as shown in the *Leg Layout*. Cut this taper in the *inside*

surfaces, using a table saw or a band saw. Joint or plane the sawed surface smooth.

7 **Cut the molding and the glue blocks.** Using a table saw, cut a chamfer in the molding strips, as shown in the *Molding Profile*. Make enough molding for both the table and the writing box.

Also bevel the edges of the glue block stock at 45 degrees on the table saw, then rip long, triangular strips. Cut these strips into 2 1/2-inch lengths to make the glue blocks, as shown in the *Glue Block Detail*.

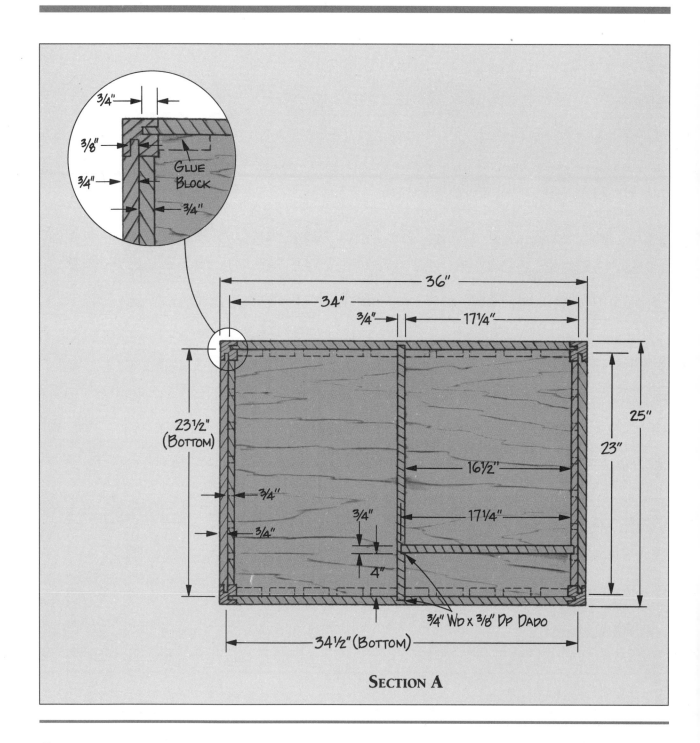

3/4"

3/8"

3/4"

GLUE
BLOCK

3/4"

36"

34"

3/4"   17¼"

23½"
(BOTTOM)

25"

23"

16½"

3/4"

3/4"

17¼"

3/4"

4"

¾" WD x ⅜" DP DADO

34½" (BOTTOM)

SECTION A

8 Cut notches in the table bottom. The corners of the table bottom are notched to fit around the legs, as shown in *Section A* and the *Table Bottom Notch Detail.* Cut these notches with a saber saw, a hand saw, or a coping saw.

9 Drill screw pockets in the back apron and spacers. The tabletop is attached to the back apron

and spacers with screws in screw pockets, as shown in the *Table Joinery Detail.* Drill these pockets in the inside surfaces of the back apron and the spacers. To make a screw pocket, drill a ½-inch-diameter counterbore first, then a ³/₁₆-inch-diameter shank hole, boring both holes 15 degrees off vertical. **Note:** The shank hole is slightly larger than the screw shank to let the top expand and contract.

10 **Assemble the tabletop and lids.** Fasten the breadboard ends to the lids with roundhead wood screws and flat washers, driving the screws through the slots in the breadboard ends as shown in the *Lid Joinery Detail.* Do *not* glue the breadboard ends to the lids; just let the screws hold them in place.

Glue rectangular wooden plugs in the mortises to cover the screw heads. The end grain of these plugs must face *out.* The plugs make the lid assemblies look as if the breadboard ends were attached with mortises and tenons, as old-time country cabinetmakers once did. However, the old-time joinery restricted wood movement causing the parts to split; these hidden screws and slots let the lids expand and contract.

Mortise the edges of the tabletop and the lids for hinges, and hinge the lids to the tabletop. Check that the lids move freely on their hinges, then disassemble the lids and the tabletop and set the hardware aside.

11 **Assemble the table.** Finish sand the tabletop, lids, aprons, legs, spacers, dividers, and table bottom. Glue the aprons to the legs. While the glue is still wet, turn the assembly upside down on the workbench and fit the bottom between the legs and aprons, resting it on the benchtop. This will keep the assembly square while the glue hardens.

Drill 3/16-inch-diameter, 1-inch-deep holes in the legs, through the mortise-and-tenon joints, as shown in the *Leg-to-Apron Joinery Detail.* Using a pocket knife or a bench knife, carve the pegs as shown in the *Peg Detail,* rounding one end. Apply a little glue to each peg, then drive it into a hole in a leg, round end first. The square end should show on the outside. This technique of driving a square peg into a round hole was used by many old-time country cabinetmakers to lock tenons in mortises.

Remove the bottom from between the legs, then glue the spacers and dividers in place. Make sure that the tops of these parts are flush with the top edges of the aprons.

Turn the top upside down on your workbench and position the table assembly over it. Attach the top to the back apron and spacers with flathead wood screws, driving the screws through the screw pockets. Fit the bottom to the assembly, resting it on the bottom edges of the spacers and dividers. Hold it in place with glue blocks, adhering these blocks to both the aprons and the bottom as shown in the *Table Joinery Detail.*

Turn the table right side up and attach the lids to the top with hinges. Don't cut or attach the molding yet — wait until after you've made the writing box.

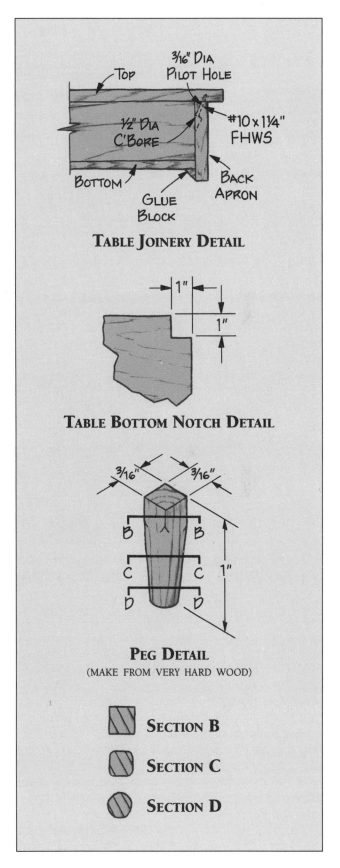

TABLE JOINERY DETAIL

TABLE BOTTOM NOTCH DETAIL

PEG DETAIL
(MAKE FROM VERY HARD WOOD)

SECTION B

SECTION C

SECTION D

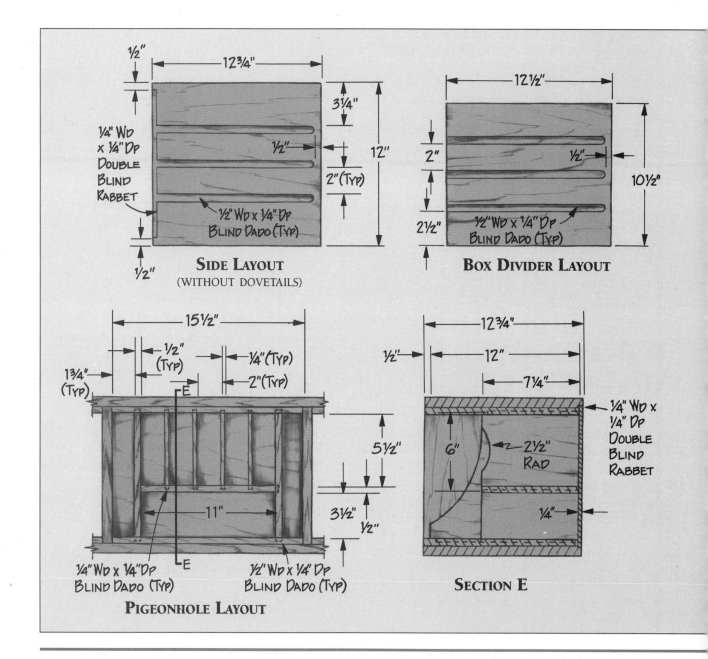

SIDE LAYOUT
(WITHOUT DOVETAILS)

BOX DIVIDER LAYOUT

PIGEONHOLE LAYOUT

SECTION E

MAKING THE WRITING BOX

12 Cut the writing box parts to size. From the ³/₄-inch-thick stock, cut the writing box top, bottom, sides, and box dividers according to the Materials List. Cut the back from ¼-inch plywood. Resaw some of the remaining ³/₄-inch-thick stock and plane it to ¼ inch. Cut the pigeonhole dividers to size, and set aside the rest of the ¼-inch-thick stock to make the drawer sides and backs. However, *don't* cut the drawer parts to size yet — wait until you've assembled the writing box and can measure the openings.

Plane the remaining ³/₄-inch-thick stock to ½ inch, and cut the shelves and spacers. Set aside some ½-inch-thick stock to make the doors, but don't cut them to size yet. Plane enough ½-inch-thick stock to ³/₈ inch to make the drawer fronts, but — once again — don't cut them to size yet.

13 Cut dovetail joints in the box top, bottom, and sides. The top, bottom, and sides of the writing box are joined with dovetail joints. Lay out the

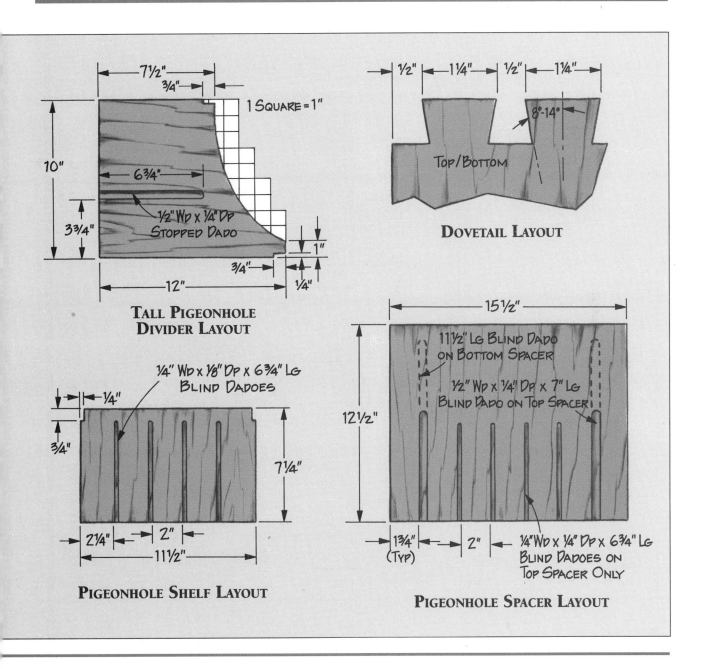

TALL PIGEONHOLE DIVIDER LAYOUT

7½"
¾"
1 Square = 1"
10"
6¾"
½" WD x ¼" DP STOPPED DADO
3¾"
1"
¾"
¼"
12"

DOVETAIL LAYOUT

½" 1¼" ½" 1¼"
8°-14°
Top/Bottom

PIGEONHOLE SHELF LAYOUT

¼" WD x ⅛" DP x 6¾" LG BLIND DADOES
¼"
¾"
7¼"
2¼" 2"
11½"

PIGEONHOLE SPACER LAYOUT

15½"
11½" LG BLIND DADO ON BOTTOM SPACER
½" WD x ¼" DP x 7" LG BLIND DADO ON TOP SPACER
12½"
1¾" (TYP) 2"
¼" WD x ¼" DP x 6¾" LG BLIND DADOES ON TOP SPACER ONLY

dovetails as shown in the *Dovetail Layout,* then cut them with a router, table saw, band saw, or dovetail saw. You can substitute finger joints or rabbet joints for the dovetails.

14 **Cut dadoes and rabbets in the writing box parts.** Most of the parts in the writing box are assembled with dadoes and rabbets. Cut these joints using a router or a dado cutter:

■ ½-inch-wide, ¼-inch-deep blind dadoes in the sides and box dividers to hold the shelves, as shown in the *Side Layout* and *Box Divider Layout*

■ ½-inch-wide, ¼-inch-deep blind dadoes in the tall pigeonhole dividers to hold the pigeonhole shelf, as shown in the *Tall Pigeonhole Divider Layout*

■ ½-inch-wide, ¼-inch-deep blind dadoes in pigeonhole spacers to hold the tall dividers, as shown in the *Pigeonhole Spacer Layout* — note that these dadoes are a different length in the top spacer than in the bottom spacer

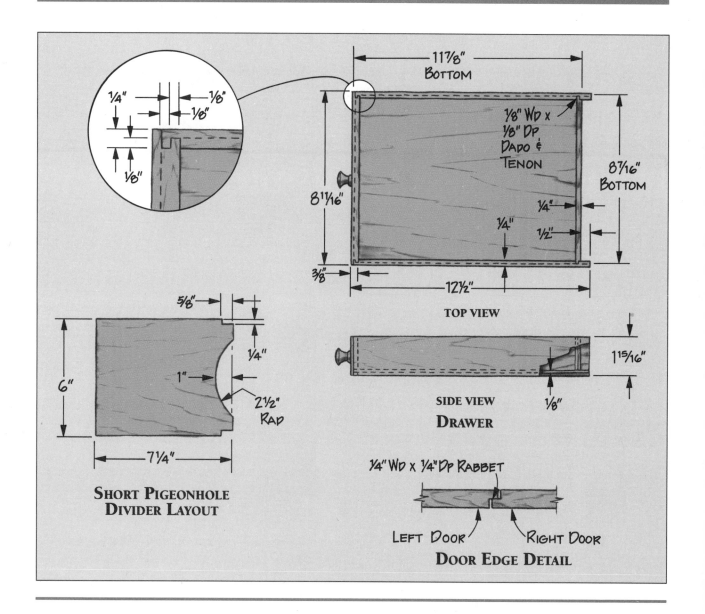

TOP VIEW

SIDE VIEW
DRAWER

SHORT PIGEONHOLE DIVIDER LAYOUT

DOOR EDGE DETAIL

■ ¹/₄-inch-wide, ¹/₄-inch-deep dadoes in the top pigeonhole spacer and the pigeonhole shelf, as shown in the *Pigeonhole Spacer Layout* and the *Pigeonhole Shelf Layout* — the dadoes are blind in the spacer and the shelf

■ ¹/₄-inch-wide, ¹/₄-inch-deep double-blind rabbets in the back edges of the top, bottom, and sides to hold the back — stop each rabbet ¹/₂ inch from each end, as shown in the *Side Layout,* then square the blind ends with a chisel

15 Cut the shapes of the shelves and dividers. Most of the front corners of the shelves and dividers are notched to fit the blind dadoes in the adjoining parts. In addition, the pigeonhole dividers are cut to

a shape. Mark ¹/₄-inch-wide, ³/₄-inch-deep notches on the front corners of the shelves, and lay out the notches and shapes of the pigeonhole shelf and dividers as shown in the *Pigeonhole Shelf Layout, Tall Pigeonhole Divider Layout,* and *Short Pigeonhole Divider Layout.* Cut the notches and shapes with a band saw or coping saw, and sand the sawed edges.

TRY THIS TRICK

To save time, stick the dividers together face to face with double-sided carpet tape, then saw and sand them as a single unit. Afterwards, take them apart and discard the tape.

16 Assemble the writing box. Finish sand the top, bottom, sides, back, shelves, and dividers. Assemble the top, bottom, and sides with glue. Before the glue dries, tack the back in place temporarily with wire brads to hold the assembly square.

Remove the back, and glue the spacers and dividers to the inside surfaces of the top and bottom. Spread glue in the dadoes that hold the shelves, and slide the shelves into place. Repeat for the tall dividers, pigeonhole shelf, and short dividers, in that order. As you assemble the shelves and dividers, use a wet rag to clean up any glue that squeezes out of the joints.

Let the glue dry, then tack the back in place with wire brads. It's not necessary to glue the back in place.

17 Cut the drawer parts. Measure the drawer openings in the assembled writing box and compare them to the measurements on the drawings. If they have changed, adjust the drawer dimensions to compensate and cut the drawer parts. Make the bottoms from ⅛-inch plywood, and the remaining parts from solid stock that you have set aside.

TRY THIS TRICK

Make the drawers precisely the same size as the drawer openings. They'll be too big to work properly, but you can sand or plane just a little stock from the outside surfaces to get a perfect fit.

---

18 Cut the drawer joinery. The drawer fronts are joined to the sides with lock joints. To make these joints, cut ⅛-inch-wide, ¼-inch-deep grooves in the ends of the drawer fronts. Each groove will create two tenons, one on either side. Cut the *back* tenon so it's just ⅛ inch long. Cut ⅛-inch-wide, ⅛-inch-deep dadoes in the sides to hold these tenons, as shown in the *Drawer/Top View.*

The backs are joined with rabbet-and-dado joints — cut ⅛-inch-wide, ⅛-inch-deep rabbets in the ends of the drawer backs, creating ⅛-inch-thick tenons. Then make ⅛-inch-wide, ⅛-inch-deep dadoes in the sides to fit the tenons. Also cut ⅛-inch-wide, ⅛-inch-deep grooves in the inside faces of the drawer fronts and sides to hold the drawer bottoms.

When you're finished cutting, drill holes in the drawer fronts to hold the pulls.

19 Assemble and fit the drawers. Finish sand the drawer parts. Glue the drawer fronts, sides, and

backs together. Before the glue dries, slide the bottoms into their grooves to hold the drawers square. After the glue dries, tack the bottoms to the drawer backs with wire nails. Sand the joints clean and flush, and attach the pulls.

Test fit the drawers in their openings. If the fit is tight, or if a drawer binds, plane or sand the outside surfaces until it slides easily in and out of the writing box.

20 Cut and hang the doors. Search the remaining ½-inch-thick stock for some quarter-sawn stock — lumber in which the annual rings run face to face. (*SEE FIGURE 6-1.*) Even though you've probably purchased plain-sawn lumber (in which the rings run edge to edge), there often are a few pieces of quarter-sawn mixed in. If you can find some, make the doors from it. If you can't, glue up some quarter-sawn stock as shown in *FIGURE 3-21* on page 50.

Measure the door opening in the writing box. If the size has changed from what is shown, adjust the door dimensions to compensate and cut them to size. Make ¼-inch-wide, ¼-inch-deep rabbets in the inside edges of the doors, as shown in the *Door Edge Detail.* This will allow the doors to lap when they close.

Finish sand the doors. Mortise the right door (the door that laps over the other one) for a cabinet lock near the upper left corner. Mortise the edges of the doors and the faces of the dividers for hinges. Attach the doors to the writing box and install the lock.

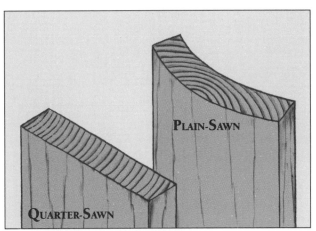

6-1 Make the doors from quarter-sawn stock. The annual rings run face to face in this kind of lumber, and it's less likely to warp than plain-sawn lumber, in which the rings run edge to edge. This will help keep the slab door flat.

PLAIN-SAWN

QUARTER-SAWN

21 Attach the moldings. Cut the moldings to fit around the top and bottom of the writing box, mitering the adjoining ends. Finish sand the moldings, then glue the top front molding to the front edge of the box, and glue the mitered ends of the top side moldings to the top front molding. However, do *not* glue the side moldings to the sides. Instead, attach them with finishing nails. The nails will bend slightly as the sides expand and contract.

Attach the bottom moldings in a similar fashion. Glue the front bottom molding to the tabletop, then glue the mitered ends of the bottom side moldings to the bottom front molding but *not* to the tabletop. Instead, attach the side moldings with finishing nails. Do *not* glue or nail any of the bottom moldings to the writing box, so you can remove the box from the table.

22 Finish the desk. Remove the lids from the table and the drawers and doors from the writing box. Set aside the metal hardware — hinges, screws, and lock. Also, take the writing box off the table.

Do any necessary touch-up sanding, then apply a finish to all wooden surfaces, inside and out. You can use almost any finish, but the project shown has an antique finish. The surface of the wood was lightly *distressed* — dented here and there with keys on a key ring — to simulate wear and tear. Next, it was sprayed with a red mahogany lacquer. When the lacquer dried, the edges and the lids were lightly sanded to look as if part of the finish had worn away. Finally, the wood was wiped with a dark walnut *glaze* — a thick stain that filled the dents and cracks and made them look as if they had collected a century or two of grime.

After finishing the desk, put the writing box back on the table. Replace the lids, drawers, doors, and hardware.

VARIATIONS

You can adapt this design to make a country-style *computer* desk. Enlarge the table slightly to provide a larger work surface, and enlarge the writing box to hold the monitor and the CPU in the center cupboard, as shown. Instead of hinging the work surface so it folds up, hinge the front apron so it folds down. Mount a sliding shelf inside the table for the keyboard. Make a separate (but matching) country cupboard with a sliding shelf to hold the printer.

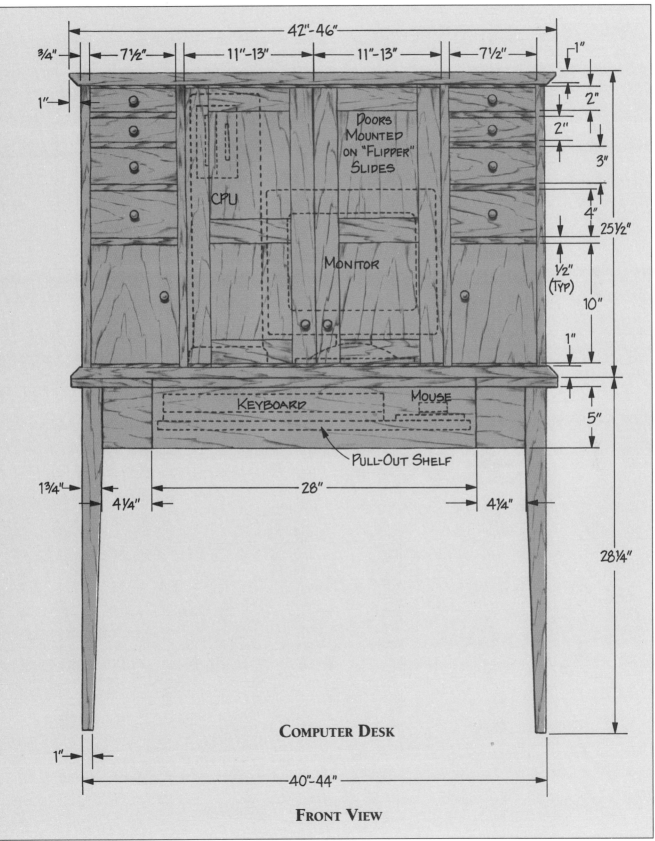

Computer Desk

Front View

(continued) ▷

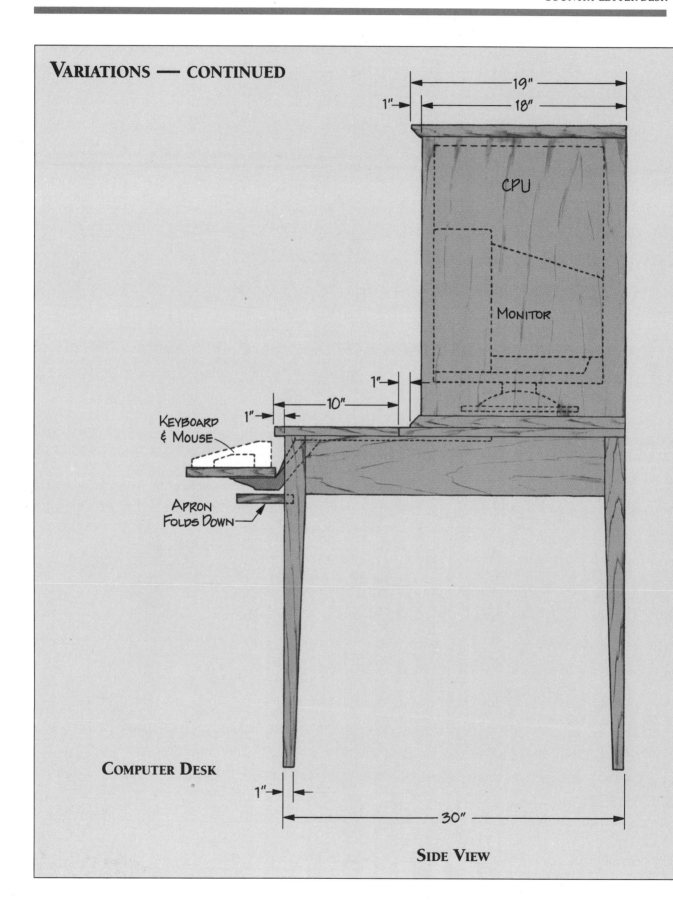

VARIATIONS — CONTINUED

19"

1"   18"

CPU

Monitor

1"

1"   10"

KEYBOARD
& MOUSE

APRON
FOLDS DOWN

COMPUTER DESK

1"

30"

SIDE VIEW

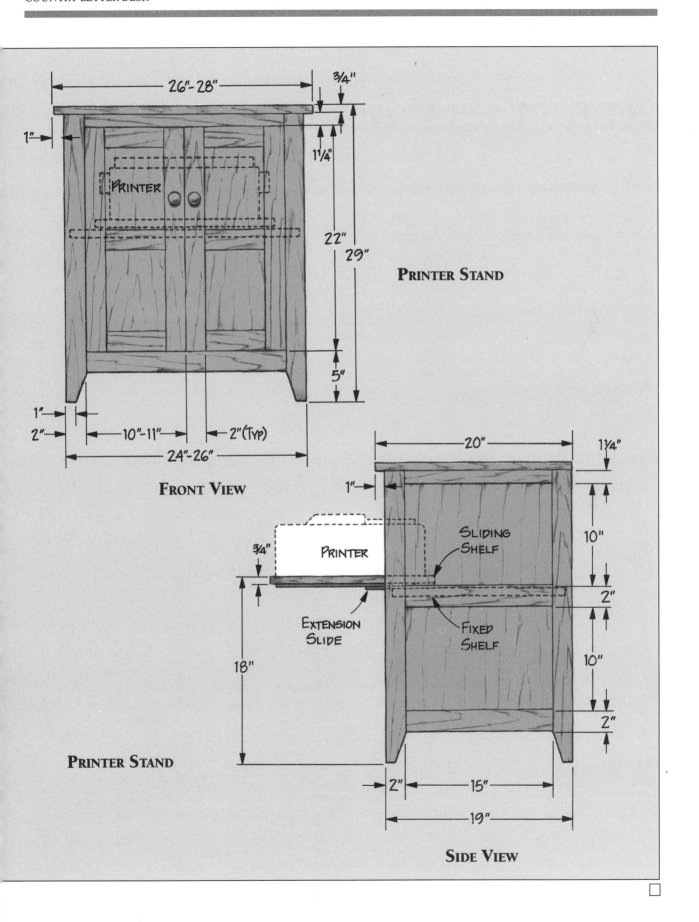

PRINTER STAND

FRONT VIEW

PRINTER STAND

SIDE VIEW

7

ADJUSTABLE BOOKSHELVES

Simple pieces can be elegant. This standing bookcase is a basic, functional case construction — just a top, a bottom, two sides, and a face frame. However, its pleasant proportions, highly grained lumber, and fine finish make this a showpiece.

As shown, the bookcase stands waist high, with two adjustable shelves. However, you can easily change the dimensions, making it taller or wider to suit your own needs. You can also change the style by modifying the decorations and overall shape. Refer to "Variations" at the end of this chapter.

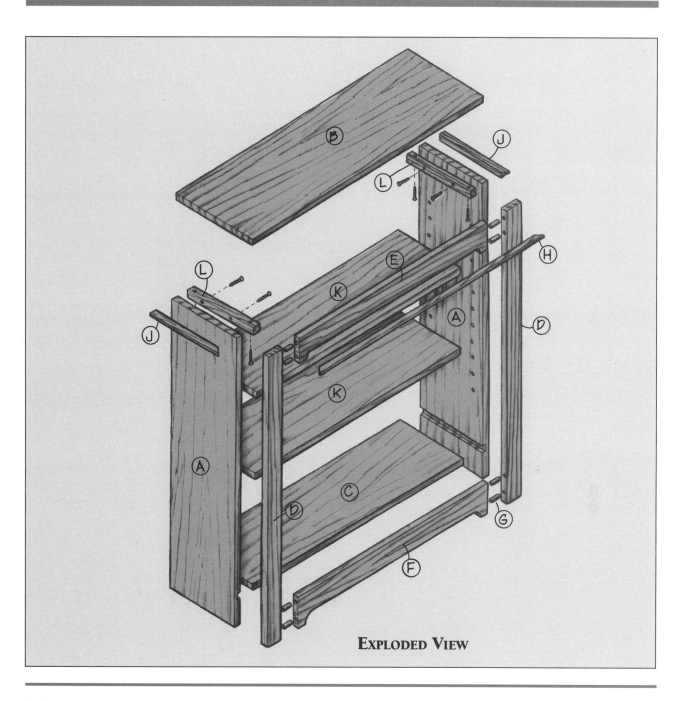

EXPLODED VIEW

MATERIALS LIST (FINISHED DIMENSIONS)

Parts

A. Sides (2)   3/4″ x 9½″ x 35¼″
B. Top   3/4″ x 11¼″ x 34″
C. Bottom   3/4″ x 9½″ x 31¼″
D. Stiles (2)   3/4″ x 2″ x 35¼″
E. Top rail   3/4″ x 3″ x 28″
F. Bottom rail   3/4″ x 4″ x 28″
G. Dowels (8)   3/8″ dia. x 2″

H. Front
    molding   3/4″ x 3/4″ x 33½″
J. Side
    moldings (2)   3/4″ x 3/4″ x 11″
K. Adjustable
    shelves (2)   3/4″ x 9½″ x 30 3/8″
L. Cleats (2)   3/4″ x 3/4″ x 9½″

Hardware

#8 x 1¼″ Flathead wood screws
(8)
7/8″ Wire brads (8–10)
¼″ dia. x 1″ Shelving support pins
(8)

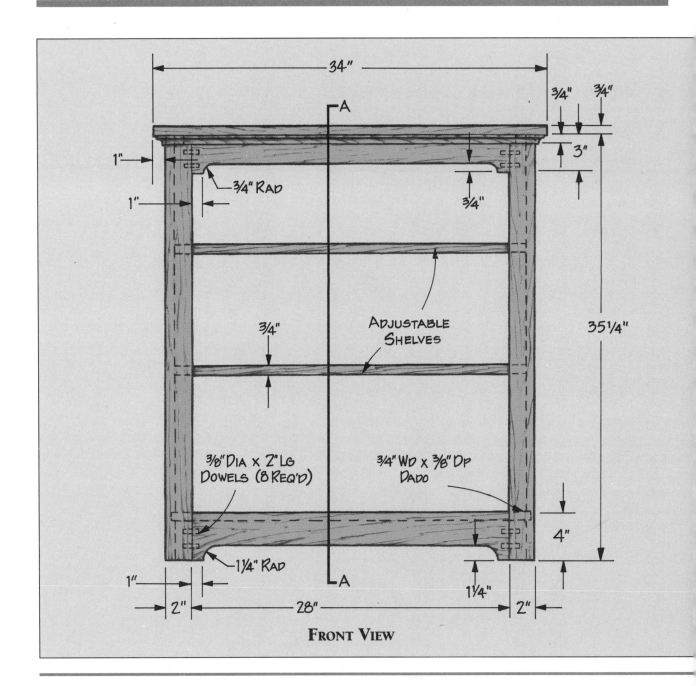

FRONT VIEW

PLAN OF PROCEDURE

1 **Select the stock and cut the parts to size.**
To build the adjustable bookcase as shown, you need about 18 board feet of 4/4 (four-quarters) stock. The bookcase shown is built from curly cherry, although you can use any cabinet-grade wood. You may also substitute plywood for the sides, top, bottom, and shelves, provided you face the visible edges to hide the plies. Plywood shelves, however, won't support as much weight as solid wood.

Plane the stock to ¾ inch thick and cut all the parts except the moldings to the sizes shown in the Materials List. Set aside some stock to make the moldings, but don't cut them yet.

2 **Cut dadoes in the sides.** The bottom rests in ¾-inch-wide, ⅜-inch-deep dadoes in the sides, as shown in the *Front View*. Cut these dadoes with a router or a dado cutter.

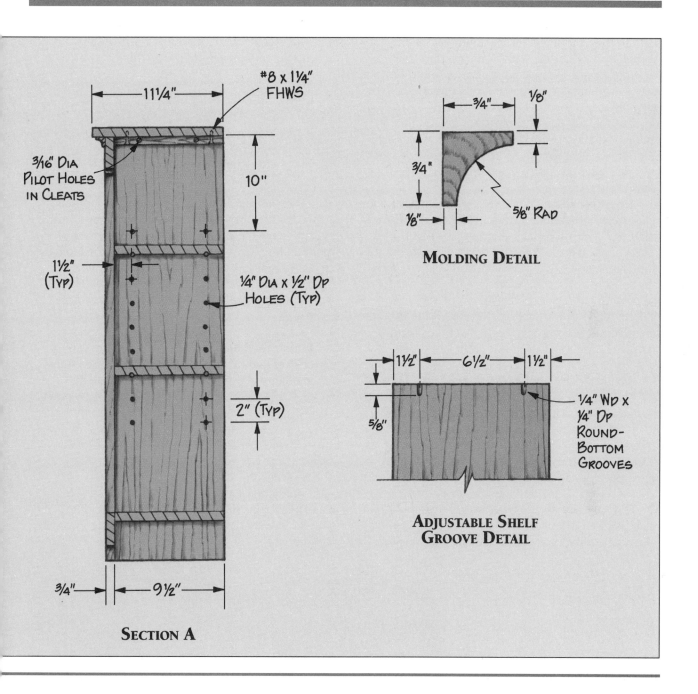

**#8 x 1¼"
FHWS**

**3/16" Dia
Pilot Holes
in Cleats**

11¼"

10"

**1½"
(Typ)**

**¼" Dia x ½" Dp
Holes (Typ)**

2" (Typ)

¾"   **9½"**

Section A

¾"   **1/8"**

¾"

1/8"   **5/8" Rad**

Molding Detail

1½"   **6½"**   **1½"**

5/8"

**¼" Wd x
¼" Dp
Round-
Bottom
Grooves**

**Adjustable Shelf
Groove Detail**

3 **Drill holes in the sides and cleats.**   The adjustable shelves rest on pin-style supports, which fit in ¼-inch-diameter, ½-inch-deep holes in the sides, as shown in *Section A*. Lay out the locations of these holes on the inside faces of the sides and drill them on a drill press. Or, bore them with a hand-held drill, using a stop collar to control the depth of the holes and a pegboard template to space the holes evenly. This template is shown in *Figure 3-11* on page 45.

Also drill countersinks and ³/₁₆-inch-diameter shank holes in the cleats. Make two sets of holes in each cleat — vertical and horizontal — to attach it to the top and one side. **Note:** The shank holes are slightly larger than the shanks of the screws to let the top and sides expand and contract.

4 **Rout the grooves in the adjustable shelves.** The adjustable shelves rest on round metal support pins. To keep the shelves from sliding off the pins, the bottom faces of the shelves are grooved, and these grooves fit over the pins. Cut the round-bottom grooves with a table-mounted router. (*See Figure 7-1*.)

5 **Cut the shapes of the rails.** Lay out the profiles of the top and bottom rail, as shown in the *Front View*. Cut the profiles with a band saw or saber saw, then sand the sawed edges.

6 **Assemble the face frame.** Mark the positions of the dowels that hold the face frame rails and stiles together, then drill 3/8-inch-diameter, 1 1/16-inch-deep holes at each mark. (The extra depth leaves room for glue.) Use a doweling jig to help guide the bit. You may substitute biscuits, splines, or loose tenons for the dowels.

Lightly sand the surfaces of the rails and stiles, then assemble the face frame with glue. Let the glue dry completely, and sand the joints clean and flush.

7 **Assemble the bookcase.** Finish sand the sides, top, bottom, and face frame. Assemble the sides, bottom, and face frame with glue. After the glue dries, attach the cleats to the sides with flathead wood screws. Remember, the top surfaces of the cleats must be flush with the top ends of the sides. Lay the top across the sides and fasten it to the cleats with screws.

8 **Cut and attach the moldings.** Select a 3/4-inch-thick board, 3 inches wide or wider, and long enough to make the moldings. Cut a 5/8-inch-radius cove in

both edges with a table-mounted router or a shaper, then rip the moldings from the board.

> ## A Safety Reminder
>
> *Don't* try to rip the molding stock to width before cutting the coves. The narrow stock may break or splinter as you shape it.

Cut the moldings to length, mitering the adjoining ends. Glue the front molding to the face frame, and glue the mitered ends of the side moldings to the front molding. However, do *not* glue the side moldings to the sides. Instead, attach them with wire brads. The brads will bend slightly as the sides expand and contract. **Note:** Don't glue either molding to the top.

9 **Finish the bookcase.** Finish sand the adjustable shelves and do any necessary touch-up sanding on the other wooden parts. Apply a finish to all wooden surfaces, inside and out. The bookcase shown is finished with a mixture of spar varnish and tung-seed oil (2 tablespoons of varnish to 1 cup of oil), although you can use any finish you wish. **Note:** *Tungseed oil* is the generic name for any wipe-on, tung-oil-based finish.

After the finish dries and you have rubbed it out, install metal pins in the holes where you want to hang the shelves. Rest the shelves so their grooves fit over the pins.

7-1 To cut the half-round grooves in the ends of the adjustable shelves, mount a 1/4-inch-diameter veining bit in a table-mounted router. Adjust the depth of cut to 1/4 inch, and position the fence 1 1/2 inches *behind* the bit. Fasten a stop to the fence, 1/2 inch to the right of the bit. With the router running, feed the shelf into the bit until it hits the stop. Turn the shelf end for end and cut another groove. Cut half of the grooves in the shelves with this setup, then move the stop 1/2 inch to the left of the bit and cut the other grooves.

VARIATIONS

Although simple, this bookcase design is extremely versatile. Not only can you build it almost any size that you need but also any *style,* simply by chang-ing the shape of a few parts. For some styles, you may wish to add or subtract pieces.

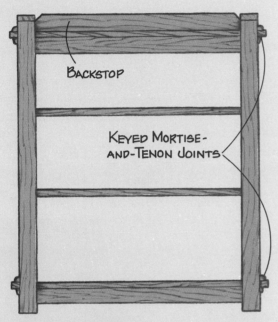

BACKSTOP

KEYED MORTISE-AND-TENON JOINTS

MISSION

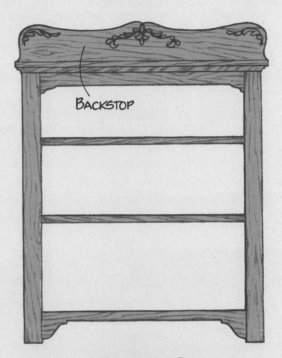

BACKSTOP

VICTORIAN OAK

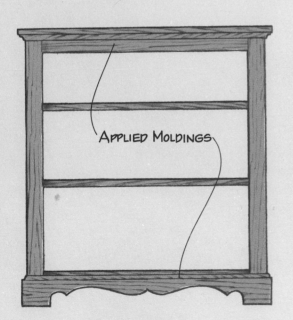

APPLIED MOLDINGS

QUEEN ANNE

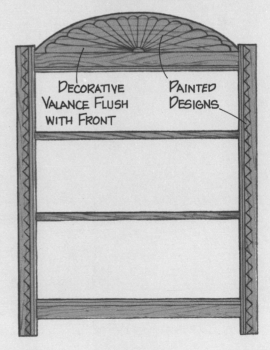

DECORATIVE VALANCE FLUSH WITH FRONT

PAINTED DESIGNS

SOUTHWEST

8

LAP DESK

Although lap desks are rarely used for writing nowadays, they remain quite useful. In an office or den, a lap desk will organize stationery, coupons, bills, and correspondence. (The compartments inside this desk are sized to hold paper and envelopes.) In other areas of the home, it can be used to store small items.

On the project shown, the base and the lid are framed, a common construction method for old lap desks and writing boxes. Frequently, the panels in the lid frames were covered with felt or leather to provide a better writing surface — especially if the writing was done with a quill pen. On the desk shown, the panel is veneered to match the wood frame.

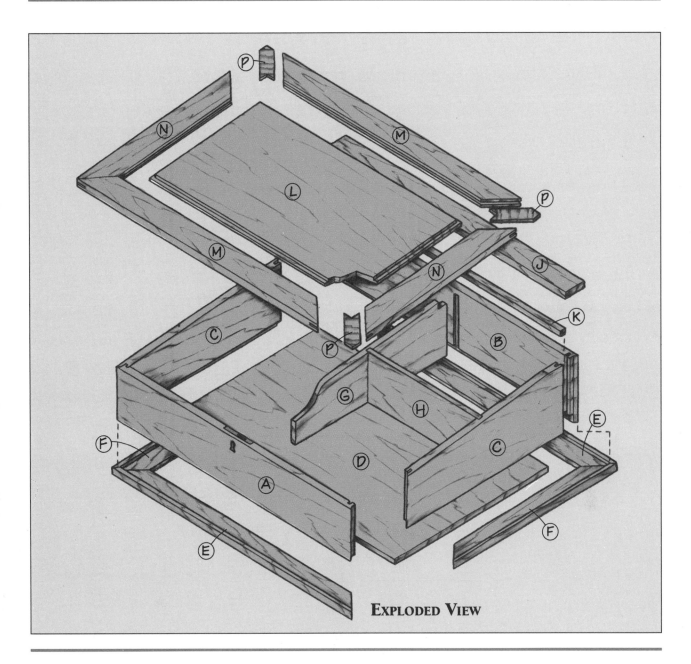

EXPLODED VIEW

MATERIALS LIST (FINISHED DIMENSIONS)

Parts

A. Front   1/2" x 3 3/4" x 19"

B. Back   1/2" x 4 3/4" x 19"

C. Sides (2)   1/2" x 4 3/4" x 13"

D. Bottom*   3/8" x 12 3/4" x 18 3/4"

E. Front/back base
moldings (2)   1/2" x 1 1/2" x 19 1/2"

F. Side base
moldings (2)   1/2" x 1 1/2" x 13 1/2"

G. Long divider   3/8" x 4 1/2" x 12 1/4"

H. Short divider   3/8" x 4" x 9 1/4"

J. Top   1/2" x 1 1/2" x 19 1/2"

K. Cleat   3/8" x 3/8" x 18"

L. Lid panel*   3/8" x 9" x 16 1/2"

M. Long lid frame
members (2)   1/2" x 1 3/4" x 19 1/2"

N. Short lid frame
members (2)   1/2" x 1 3/4" x 12"

P. Splines (4)   1/8" x 2 1/2" x 1/2"

Hardware

1" x 19 1/2" Piano hinge and mounting screws

Piano lock and mounting screws

Make these parts from plywood.

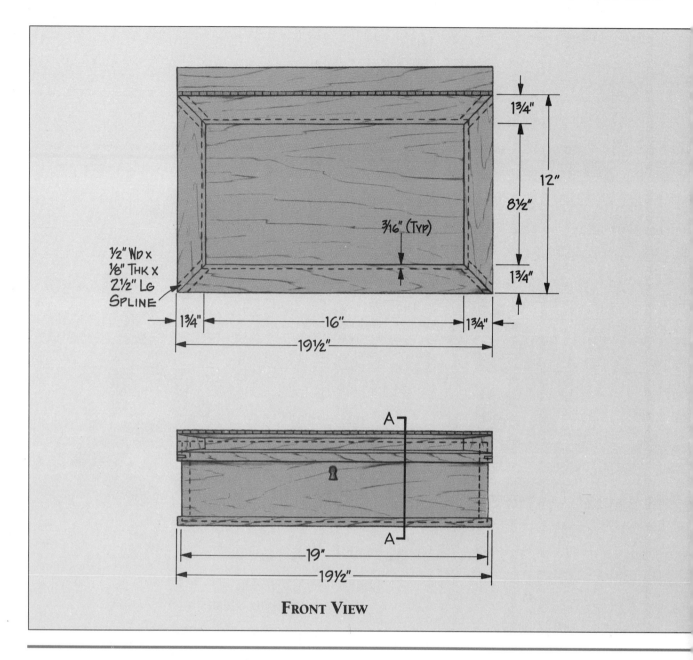

FRONT VIEW

PLAN OF PROCEDURE

1 Select the stock and cut the parts to size.
To make this project, you need approximately 6 board feet of 4/4 (four-quarters) stock and a 24-inch-square piece of cabinet-grade ³⁄₈-inch plywood. The veneer on the plywood should match or complement the solid stock. You can also use ordinary shop-grade plywood and cover it with another veneer. Or you can cover it with leather or felt, like an old-time lap desk. The lap desk shown is made from cherry and cherry-veneer plywood.

Plane the 4/4 stock to ¹⁄₂ inch thick. Cut the top to the size shown in the Materials List, beveling the front edge at 87¹⁄₂ degrees (2¹⁄₂ degrees off perpendicular). Rip the front, back, sides, base moldings, and lid frame members to the proper width, but cut them about ¹⁄₂ inch long to leave room for the miter joints. As you rip the back lid frame member, bevel the back edge at 87¹⁄₂ degrees. As you rip the front, bevel the top edge at 85 degrees (5 degrees off perpendicular) to match the slant of the lid.

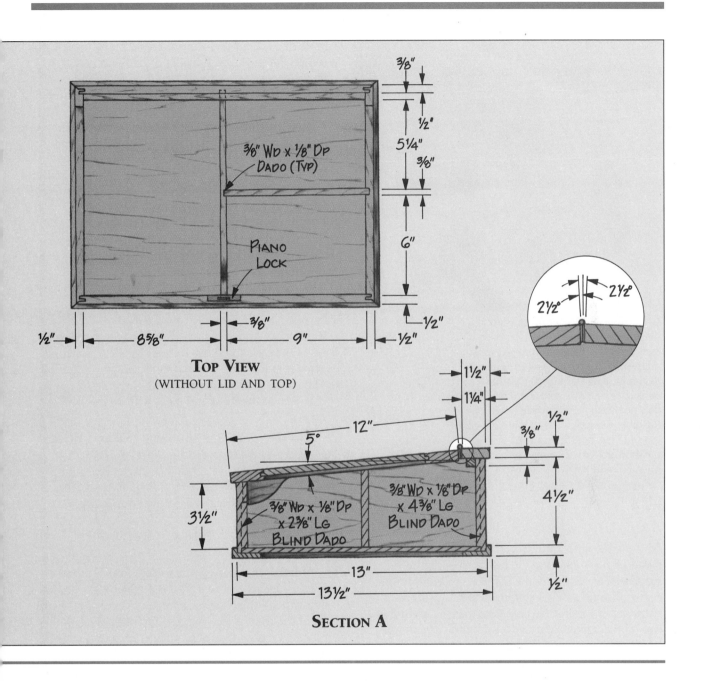

TOP VIEW
(WITHOUT LID AND TOP)

SECTION A

Set aside some 1/2-inch-thick stock to make test cuts, and plane the remainder to 3/8 inch thick. Cut the dividers and the cleats to size. As you rip the short divider, bevel the top at 85 degrees. Also, cut the lid panel and bottom from plywood.

2 **Cut the miter joints in the front, back, and sides.** As shown, the front, back, and sides are joined with *lock miters* — a combination of a lock joint and a simple miter. These must be cut with a

special router bit. (*SEE FIGURE 8-1.*) However, if you don't have the equipment needed to make them, you can substitute ordinary miter joints. You might also use through dovetails or finger joints.

3 **Cut the splined miters that join the base moldings and lid frame members.** Miter the ends of the base moldings and lid frame members. The miters that hold the lid together are *splined* to make them more durable. Using a tenoning jig to position

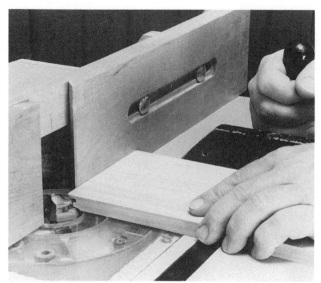

8-1 To make lock miters, you need a special router bit — *corner lock miter* bits are sold through most mail-order woodworking suppliers. When cutting the joints, pass the ends of the boards across the bit. The first board should rest face down on the table, as shown. Use a miter gauge to guide the board, and a fence to position the cut. The second board must be held vertically — use a tenoning jig to position and guide it.

and guide the frame members, cut ⅛-inch-wide, ¼-inch-deep spline grooves in the ends. These grooves should be ¼ inch from the top faces of the frame members, as shown in the *Lid Joinery Detail*. From scraps of solid stock, cut splines to fit the grooves, as shown in the *Spline Layout*. Note that the grain direction of the spline runs *across* the spline joint — *this is very important!*

> ## TRY THIS TRICK
> **U**se a *flat-ground* (chisel-tooth) rip blade to cut the spline grooves. With the exception of thin-kerf blades, most table saw blades cut ⅛-inch-wide kerfs, and you can use these for making narrow grooves and dadoes. But only a flat-ground blade will leave a flat bottom as it cuts.

4 Cut rabbets, dadoes, and grooves in the desk parts. The remaining joinery in the lap desk is simple dadoes, grooves, and rabbets. Make these with a router, flat-ground rip blade, or dado cutter:

■ ⅛-inch-wide, ¼-inch-deep grooves in the inside edges of the lid frame members to hold the lid panel, as shown in the *Lid Joinery Detail*

■ ¼-inch-wide, ¼-inch-deep rabbets in the upper edges and ends of the lid panel — these will create tongues to fit the grooves in the frame members

■ ⅜-inch-wide, ⅜-inch-deep rabbets in the bottom edges of the front, back, and sides to hold the bottom, as shown in the *Base Joinery Detail*

■ ⅜-inch-wide, ⅛-inch-deep blind dadoes in the front and back to hold the long divider — the front dado is 2⅜ inches long, and the back one is 4⅜ inches long, as shown in *Section A*

■ ⅜-inch-wide, ⅛-inch-deep dadoes in the right side and long divider to hold the short divider, as shown in the *Top View (without lid and top)*

■ 1¼-inch-wide, ¼-inch-deep rabbets in the top faces of the base moldings to hold the desk assembly, as shown in the *Base Joinery Detail*

After cutting these joints, square the blind ends of the dadoes in the front and back with a chisel.

5 Cut the profiles of the sides and long divider. The sides and the long divider taper from back to front so the lid rests at a 5-degree angle. Lay out the profiles of the sides as shown in *Section A,* and the profile of the long divider as shown in the *Long Divider Layout*. Cut the profiles with a band saw or scroll saw, then sand the sawed edges.

6 Mortise the front for a lock. Rout a mortise in the inside face of the front for a piano lock, and cut a slot through the front for a keyhole. Because the top edge of the front is beveled, the top of the lock will not be flush with the wood surface. This is okay — just make sure the back corner of the lock is even with the back arris (the highest point) of the front, as shown in the *Lock Detail.*

7 Assemble the desk box. Finish sand all the parts. Glue the base moldings together to make a frame. While the glue is drying on this frame, glue together the front, back, sides, long divider, and bottom. Let the glue set up, then glue the box assembly to the base frame. Spread glue in the dadoes that hold the short divider, and slide it into place. Glue the cleat to the inside face of the back, flush with the top edge, then glue the top to the cleat, back, and sides. Make sure the beveled edge of the top faces forward.

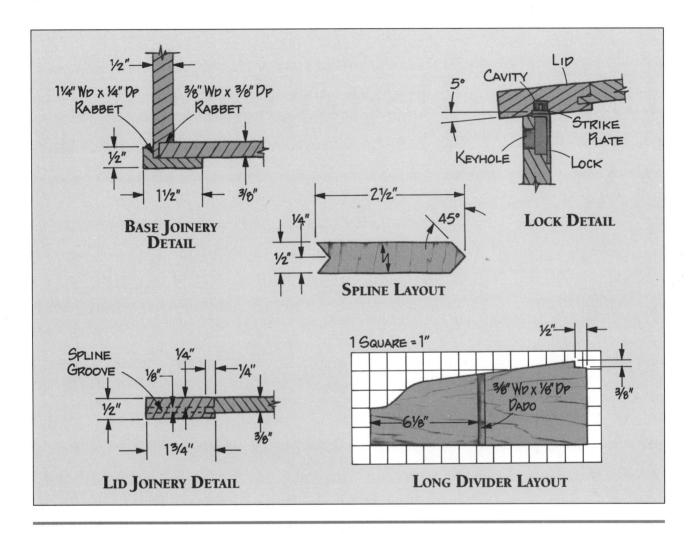

BASE JOINERY DETAIL

1¼" WD x ¼" DP RABBET
3/8" WD x 3/8" DP RABBET
½"
½"
1½"
3/8"

LOCK DETAIL

LID
CAVITY
5°
STRIKE PLATE
KEYHOLE
LOCK

SPLINE LAYOUT

2½"
¼"
½"
45°

LID JOINERY DETAIL

SPLINE GROOVE
¼"
1/8"
¼"
½"
1¾"
3/8"

LONG DIVIDER LAYOUT

1 SQUARE = 1"
½"
3/8" WD x 1/8" DP DADO
3/8"
6¼"

TRY THIS TRICK

As you clamp these glue joints together, wipe away any glue that squeezes out with a *sopping wet* rag. Be certain to wash away all the extra glue. This will raise the grain slightly, but you can easily sand the wood smooth with very fine sandpaper after the surface dries.

8 Assemble and attach the lid. Glue together the lid frame members, splines, and lid panel. Let the glue dry, then sand the joints clean and smooth. When sanding the surface of the panel, be very careful not to sand through the thin veneer.

Make sure that the sloping edges of the sides, front, and long divider are all even with one another. If not, true them up with a block plane or a file. Screw a piano hinge to the back edge (the beveled edge) of the lid assembly; then screw the hinge to the front edge of the top.

Mark the position of the striker plate on the underside of the lid assembly. Chisel out the mortise for the plate so the mortise bottom slopes 5 degrees toward the front, as shown in the *Lock Detail* — this will let the striker plate rest flat on top of the lock when the lid is closed. Install the plate and check that the lock engages it.

9 Finish the lap desk. Remove the hinge, lock, and striker plate. Set the hardware aside and do any necessary touch-up sanding. Apply a finish to all wood surfaces, inside and out. The lap desk shown was covered with multiple coats of tungseed oil (a tung-oil-based wipe-on finish), but you can use any finish you wish. When the finish dries, rub it out to the desired gloss and reassemble the desk.

9

HANGING DISPLAY CASE

When properly designed, a display case can give you a better view of the items inside than if they were out in the open. For example, this case has glass shelves to let you see beneath the objects, and a mirrored back so you can see both the fronts and backs of the objects at the same time. The interior is also lighted to help you see better.

This particular display case also includes some ordinary cupboard space. Underneath the glazed doors are two small wooden doors that swing down to reveal space for items you *don't* want to display. For example, if you displayed musical instruments behind the glazed doors, you might keep sheet music behind the wooden ones.

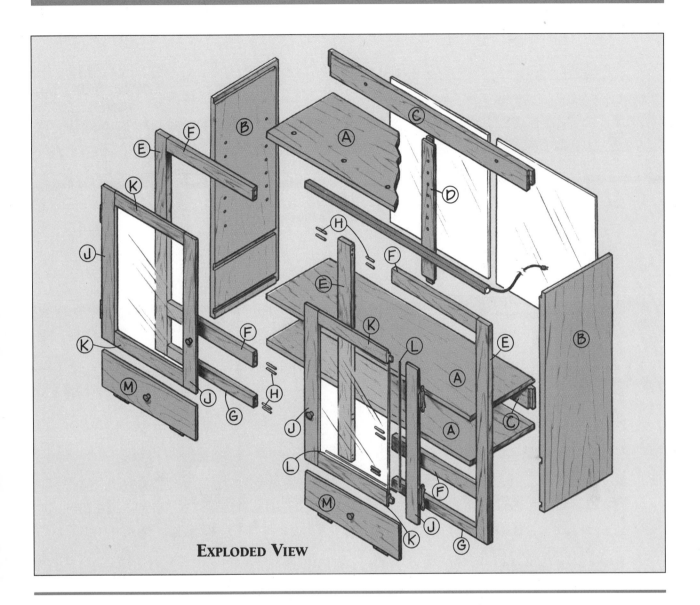

EXPLODED VIEW

MATERIALS LIST (FINISHED DIMENSIONS)

Parts

A. Fixed
   shelves (3)   ³/₄″ x 11¹/₄″ x 35¹/₄″

B. Sides (2)   ³/₄″ x 11¹/₄″ x 32″

C. Back rails (2)   ³/₄″ x 3″ x 35¹/₄″

D. Middle back
   stile   ³/₄″ x 2″ x 21¹/₄″

E. Face frame
   stiles (3)   ³/₄″ x 2″ x 32″

F. Upper face frame
   rails (4)   ³/₄″ x 2″ x 15″

G. Lower face frame
   rails (2)   ³/₄″ x 1¹/₂″ x 15″

H. Dowels (24)   ¹/₄″ dia. x 1¹/₄″

J. Upper door
   stiles (4)   ³/₄″ x 2″ x 22⁵/₈″

K. Upper door
   rails (4)   ³/₄″ x 2″ x 13⁷/₈″

L. Glass bead
   (total)   ³/₈″ x ³/₈″ x 132″

M. Lower
   doors (2)   ³/₄″ x 5¹/₈″ x 15⁵/₈″

Hardware

¹/₄″ x 17″ x 21¹/₄″ Mirrors (2)

¹/₄″ x 10″ x 34¹/₈″ Glass shelf

¹/₈″ x 12¹/₄″ x 19¹/₄″ Glass panes
   for doors (2)

¹/₂″ Wire brads (48–60)

Rubber-coated shelving support
   pins (6)

Self-closing offset hinges and
   mounting screws (4 pairs)

Door pulls (4)

30″ Light strip and mounting
   hardware

¹/₄″ x 3″ Lag screws to hang case (4)

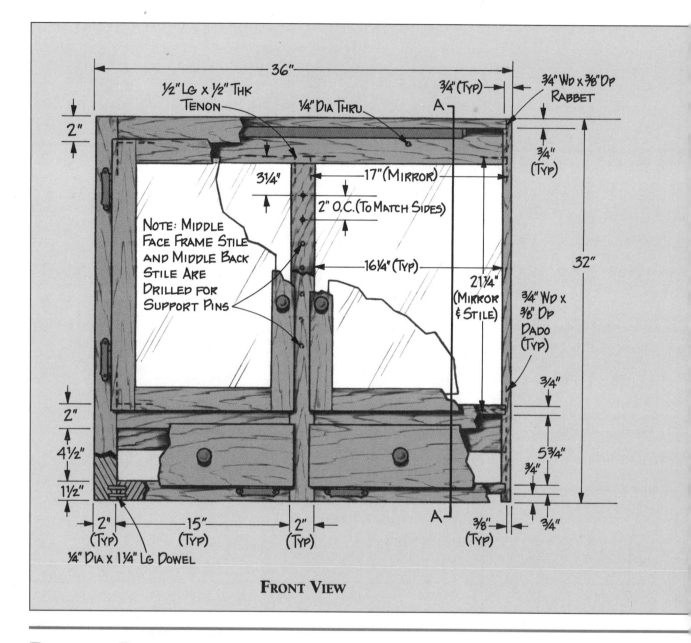

FRONT VIEW

PLAN OF PROCEDURE

1 Select the stock and cut the parts to size.
To build this project as shown, you'll need about 25
board feet of 4/4 (four-quarters) stock and a 36-inch
length of ¼-inch-diameter dowel stock. The display
case pictured is made from wavy birch, but you can
use almost any cabinet-grade wood.

Plane the 4/4 stock to ¾ inch thick and cut all the
parts to the dimensions given in the Materials List,
except for the glass beading. Select two or three
straight, clear scraps at least 3 inches wide and 20
inches long and plane them to ⅜ inch thick. Set these

aside to make the glass beading, but don't cut the
beading to size yet.

**2 Cut the joinery in the sides, upper back rail,
and middle shelf.** The parts of the case are joined
with dadoes and rabbets. Make these joints with a
router or dado cutter:

■ ¾-inch-wide, ⅜-inch-deep rabbets in the top
ends of the sides to hold the top shelf, as shown in
the *Front View*

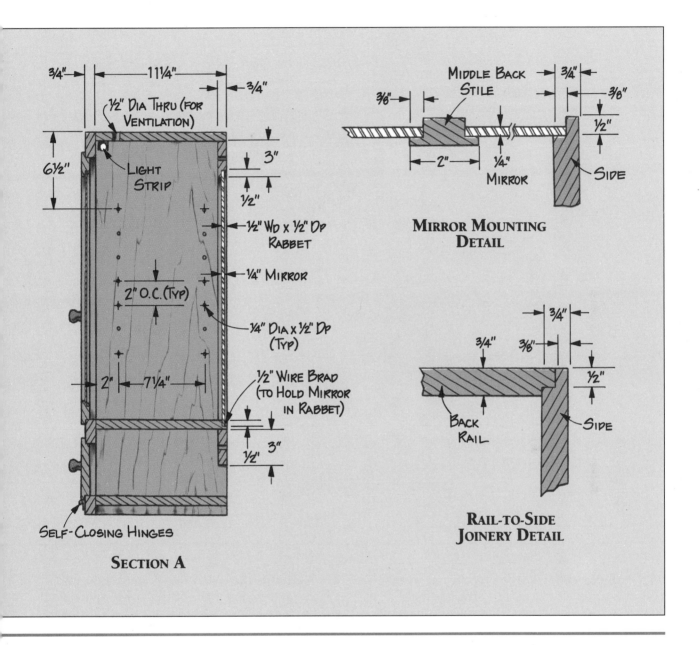

½" Dia Thru (for Ventilation)

Light Strip

3/4"   **11¼"**   **3/4"**

6½"   **3"**   **½"**

½" Wd x ½" Dp Rabbet

¼" Mirror

2" O.C. (Typ)

¼" Dia x ½" Dp (Typ)

2"   **7¼"**

½" Wire Brad (to Hold Mirror in Rabbet)

½"   **3"**

Self-Closing Hinges

SECTION A

Middle Back Stile   **3/4"**   **3/8"**

3/8"   **½"**

2"   **¼" Mirror**   **Side**

MIRROR MOUNTING DETAIL

3/4"

3/4"   **3/8"**   **½"**

Back Rail   **Side**

RAIL-TO-SIDE JOINERY DETAIL

■ ³⁄₄-inch-wide, ³⁄₈-inch-deep dadoes in the sides to hold the middle and bottom shelves

■ ³⁄₈-inch-wide, ½-inch-deep rabbets in the back edges of the sides to hold the mirrors and rails, as shown in the *Rail-to-Side Joinery Detail*

■ ³⁄₈-inch-wide, ½-inch-deep rabbets in both edges of the middle back stile to hold the mirrors, as shown in the *Mirror Mounting Detail*

■ ³⁄₈-inch-wide, ½-inch-deep rabbets in the bottom edge of the top back rail and the back edge of the middle shelf to hold the mirrors

■ ³⁄₈-inch-wide, ¼-inch-deep rabbets in the ends of the back rails and middle back stile, as shown in the *Rail-to-Side Joinery Detail*

3 **Drill holes for shelving support pins.** The adjustable glass shelves in the display case are supported by movable pins that rest in ¼-inch-diameter, ½-inch-deep holes. Drill these holes in the side, middle back stile, and middle face frame stile, as shown in the *Front View* and *Section A*.

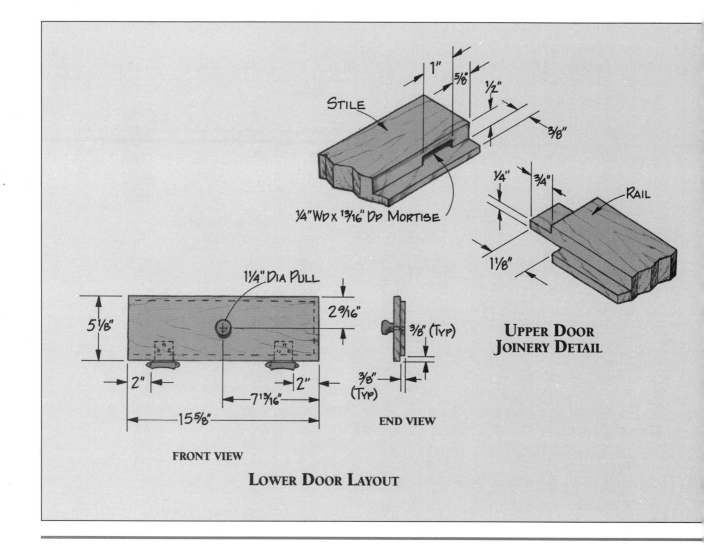

STILE

¼"WD x ¹³⁄₁₆" DP MORTISE

1"

⅝"

½"

⅜"

¼"

¾"

1⅛"

RAIL

UPPER DOOR JOINERY DETAIL

1¼" DIA PULL

2⁹⁄₁₆"

5⅛"

2"

7¹³⁄₁₆"

2"

15⅝"

3⁄8" (TYP)

3⁄8" (TYP)

END VIEW

FRONT VIEW

LOWER DOOR LAYOUT

4 Drill dowel holes in the face frame members. The rails and stiles that make up the face frame are joined with ¼-inch-diameter, 1¼-inch-long dowels, as shown in the *Front View.* Using a doweling jig to guide the drill bit, bore ¼-inch-diameter, ¹¹⁄₁₆-inch-deep holes in the ends and edges of the parts. (The extra depth leaves room for glue.) You may substitute biscuits or loose tenons for dowels.

5 Drill ventilation holes. If you plan to put a light strip in the case, you will need some ventilation holes in the top to prevent the hot air from building up inside the case. Drill ½-inch-diameter holes every 5 or 6 inches near where you will mount the light. Since these light strips don't create a great deal of heat, you probably won't need matching holes at the bottom of the case to let cool air in — enough air will flow in around the doors.

6 Assemble the case. Finish sand the parts of the case and the face frame. Glue together the sides, shelves, rails, and middle back stile, checking that the case is square as you clamp it up. Let the glue dry, then remove the clamps and rest the case on its back.

Assemble the face frame with dowels and glue. As you put the members together, rest the face frame on the front edges of the case. Before the glue dries, clamp the assembled frame to the case, making sure that all the outside edges of the frame are flush with the outside surfaces of the case. After the glue dries, the frame will fit the case perfectly.

Finally, glue the frame to the case. Sand all the joints clean and flush.

7 Make the upper door frames. The door frame members are joined with rabbeted mortises and tenons, as shown in the *Upper Door Joinery Detail.* To

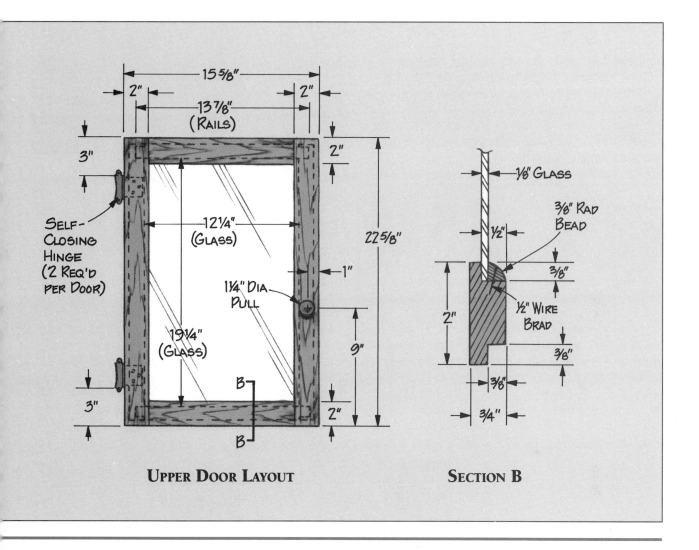

UPPER DOOR LAYOUT   **SECTION B**

make these joints, first cut ³/₈-inch-wide, ¹/₂-inch-deep rabbets in the inside edges of all the frame members. Then cut ¹/₄-inch-wide, ¹³/₁₆-inch-deep, 1-inch-long mortises near the ends of the stiles. Make ³/₄-inch-wide, ¹/₄-inch-deep rabbets in the ends of the rails on the *inside* faces, then turn the rails over and make 1¹/₈-inch-wide, ¹/₄-inch-deep rabbets on the *outside*.

Finish sand the frame members and glue them together. As you clamp them up, check that they are square.

8   Cut the lips in the doors. Both the upper and lower doors are lipped. To create the lips, cut ³/₈-inch-wide, ³/₈-inch-deep rabbets all around the outside edges of the doors.

9   Mount the doors on the case. Install self-closing offset hinges on the outside edges of the

upper doors and the bottom edges of the lower doors. Then fasten the hinges to the face frame. With the doors mounted, mark the positions of the pulls and install them.

10   Finish the case. Remove the hinges and pulls. Set the hardware aside and do any necessary touch-up sanding. Apply a finish to all wooden surfaces, inside and out. The display case shown is finished with a mixture of spar varnish and tungseed oil (2 tablespoons of varnish to 1 cup of oil), but you can use any finish you wish. After the finish dries, rub it out to the desired gloss.

11   Install the glass and the mirrors. The glass in the upper doors is held in place by wooden glass beading — small, quarter-round moldings. To make this beading, rout a ³/₈-inch-radius on the edges of the

³⁄₈-inch-thick stock you set aside for this purpose. Then rip ³⁄₈-inch-wide strips from the edges. Repeat until you have made as much beading as you need.

Cut the beading to length, mitering the ends. Lightly sand the rounded surface of the beading, and apply a finish. Let the finish dry and rub it out. Lay the panes of glass inside the door frames and tack the beading in place with wire brads, as shown in *Section B*. If necessary, touch up the finish.

Try This Trick

To prevent the brads from splitting the beading, use a 1-inch-long brad to drill pilot holes. Mount the brad in the drill chuck and spin it through the beading and into the door frame.

The mirrors are held in their rabbets with wire brads, in the same manner that you might mount a photo or a picture inside a frame. Turn the case so it rests on the face frame, lay the mirrors in place, and drive brads into the shoulders of the rabbets. Space the brads every 6 to 8 inches, and don't drive them all the way in — leave about ¼ inch showing.

Try This Trick

To keep the glass panes and the mirrors from rattling, apply a small bead of silicone inside the rabbets before you install them. Install the panes, wait for the silicone to dry, then cut away squeeze-out with a utility knife.

After the mirrors are in place, stand the case up and reinstall the doors.

12 **Hang the display case.** To mount the display case, level it on the wall and drive lag screws through the rails. If you're mounting the case on a frame wall, first locate the studs in the wall. Calculate the positions of the studs behind the case and drill ¼-inch-diameter holes through the rails at these positions. Drive the lag screws through the holes and into the studs. If you're hanging the case on a masonry wall, calculate the positions of the holes in the rails so these fall over a mortar seam between the bricks or blocks. Drill holes in the mortar at these positions and install expandable lead anchors. Then drive lag screws through the rails and into the anchors. (*SEE FIGURE 9-1.*)

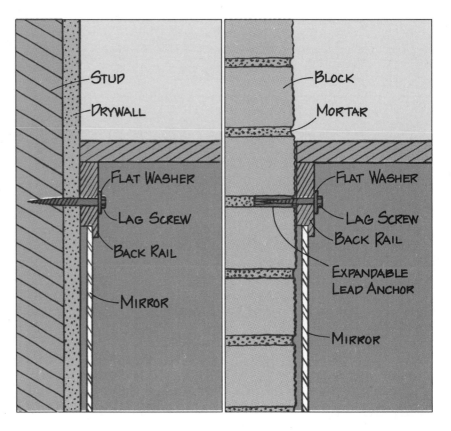

9-1 Because the display case is a fairly heavy piece, it must be solidly anchored to the wall. If you mount it on a frame wall, locate the studs and drive lag screws through the rails and into the studs. If you mount it on a masonry wall, install lead anchors between the bricks or blocks, then drive lag screws through the rails and into the anchors.

INDEX

Note: Page references in *italic* indicate photographs or illustrations.
Boldface references indicate charts or tables.

WOODWORKING GLOSSARY

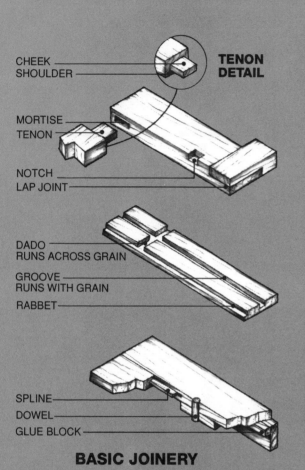

TENON DETAIL

CHEEK
SHOULDER

MORTISE
TENON

NOTCH
LAP JOINT

DADO
RUNS ACROSS GRAIN

GROOVE
RUNS WITH GRAIN

RABBET

SPLINE
DOWEL
GLUE BLOCK

BASIC JOINERY

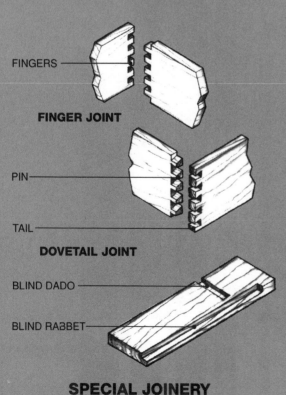

FINGER JOINT

FINGERS

PIN

TAIL

DOVETAIL JOINT

BLIND DADO

BLIND RABBET

SPECIAL JOINERY

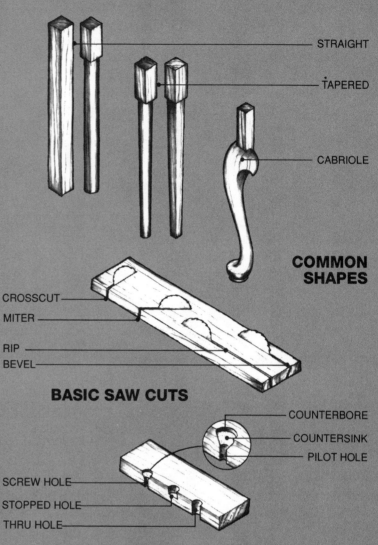

STRAIGHT

TAPERED

CABRIOLE

COMMON SHAPES

CROSSCUT

MITER

RIP

BEVEL

BASIC SAW CUTS

COUNTERBORE
COUNTERSINK
PILOT HOLE

SCREW HOLE

STOPPED HOLE

THRU HOLE

HOLES

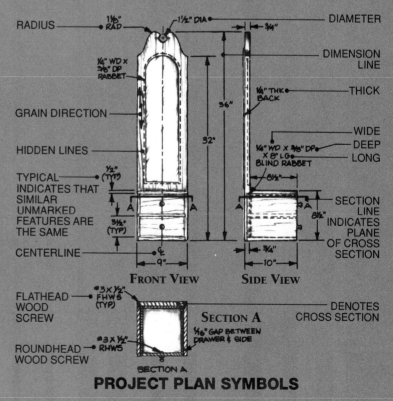

RADIUS — 1⅛" RAD   1½" DIA   ¾"   DIAMETER

¼" WD x ⅜" DP RABBET

DIMENSION LINE

36"

¼" THK BACK — THICK

32"

¼" WD x ⅜" DP X 8" LG BLIND RABBET

WIDE
DEEP
LONG

GRAIN DIRECTION

HIDDEN LINES

8½"

TYPICAL
INDICATES THAT
SIMILAR
UNMARKED
FEATURES ARE
THE SAME

½" (TYP)

A   A

A   A   8½"

SECTION
LINE
INDICATES
PLANE
OF CROSS
SECTION

3½" (TYP)

CENTERLINE

¾"

9"   10"

FRONT VIEW   **SIDE VIEW**

FLATHEAD
WOOD
SCREW

#3 X ½"
FHWS
(TYP)

SECTION A

#3 X ½"
RHWS

ROUNDHEAD
WOOD SCREW

1/16" GAP BETWEEN
DRAWER & SIDE

SECTION A

DENOTES
CROSS SECTION

PROJECT PLAN SYMBOLS